The soft petals of grace

Communion liturgies and other resources

Thom M Shuman

wild goose
publications

www.**ionabooks**.com

The soft petals of grace

Communion liturgies and other resources

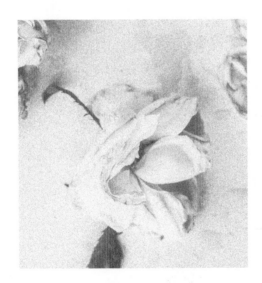

Contents

Introduction

For about a dozen years now, I have been writing liturgies and prayers for worship, and poetry and devotions for my own spiritual journey, as well as to share with others. On several occasions, I have been asked to share my writing process but have finally given up trying to explain what I find to be unexplainable. In semi-retirement, I do try to spend time each day writing, but it is never at the same time of day or in the same place. If pressed, I would describe what I do as my own form of *lectio divina*. If working with texts for a particular Sunday, I read them over and begin jotting down ideas, images, words/phrases that are jumbled in my mind. These then seem to form themselves into the elements of worship. But as I do this, I also draw on images from the day: people, events in the news, a congregation, a community to weave into the liturgy.

In the last few years, I have also been spending time with readings from a daily lectionary, which stimulate poems, prayers and devotions. In doing so, I am drawn more and more to the belief that scripture is very much alive, that the verses, stories, people, events can speak to us today, if we but listen with our hearts and souls. I am also more and more convinced that God speaks to us through all that is around and in us, if we but open ourselves more and more. These ancient words become true and alive in us when we realise that the old couple called to new ministry are on the bus next to us, that the children Jesus wants to bless are the ones fleeing their war-torn country, that the folk who hunger for healing and hope are our neighbours.

This awareness came from the time in 2001 when I had a chance to spend three and a half months away from ministry, going to places I had always dreamed about visiting – the Abbey of Gethsemani, Taizé, Iona – for the 'soul purpose' of recharging my spiritual batteries. While many experiences and people made those months transformative, because life and time slowed down considerably, I began to notice more all that is around us – lambs bouncing in fields, kids playing hopscotch on sidewalks, older folks holding hands, flowers insisting on surviving in bitter temperatures ... So much of the ordinary is *truly extraordinary*, so much of what we take for granted are the soft petals of grace strewn on the paths we walk, so much of the air we breathe is filled with wonder, hope, joy and peace. I truly discovered this in the month I spent on Iona, where the words began to tumble out, and have not stopped spilling out!

– Thom M Shuman

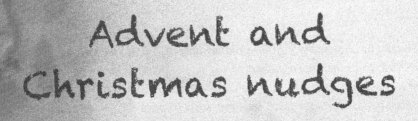

Advent and Christmas nudges

A daily discipline of Bible readings and short prayers

Introduction

It would be a lot easier if God would just trip me up, to get me to slow down in the rush to Christmas, or if God would simply deaden all the noise around me for a little while each day, so I might have space to listen. But instead, God sends a little girl loudly singing a Christmas carol; a pack of teenagers, who stop in the midst of all their twittering and texting to go talk to residents at the retirement home; grandparents who, instead of taking the family out for a big dinner, bring them down to serve at the soup kitchen …

God nudges me along the way to the manger, reminding me to stop and taste the grace, to cradle the wonder, to touch the joy, to prepare myself for that gift that comes gently, suddenly, at that precise moment we need it – especially when we are not even expecting it.

May these Advent nudges bless you on your journey to Bethlehem.

– Thom Shuman

First Sunday of Advent

*For you yourselves know very well that the day of the Lord will
come like a thief in the night.*

1 Thessalonians 5:2

You bypass
every security code
we devise
(even encrypted)
to open our hearts
and tiptoe in.

First Monday of Advent

'Tell the daughter of Zion,
Look, your king is coming to you,
humble, and mounted on a donkey,
and on a colt, the foal of a donkey.'

Matthew 21:5

Look,
our salvation is coming,
so poor as to be born in a barn,
with a donkey for a nanny.

First Tuesday of Advent

Jesus said to them, 'Yes; have you never read,
"Out of the mouths of infants and nursing babies
you have prepared praise for yourself"?'

Matthew 21:16b

Today, listen
to the carols
babbled by babies,
to the hosannas
sung by toddlers!

First Wednesday of Advent

Jesus said to them, 'Truly I tell you, the tax collectors and the prostitutes are
going into the kingdom of God ahead of you.'

Matthew 21:31b

Following
the asylum seekers,
the rough sleepers,
the innkeepers,
the street sweepers:
we find our way
into your kingdom.

First Thursday of Advent

Therefore, beloved, while you are waiting for these things, strive
to be found by him at peace, without spot or blemish; and
regard the patience of our Lord as salvation.

2 Peter 3:14–15a

In the waiting,
may we find patience;
in the patience,
may we find peace;
in the peace,
may we find you.

First Friday of Advent

Hate evil and love good,
and establish justice in the gate;
it may be that the Lord, the God of hosts,
will be gracious to the remnant of Joseph.

Amos 5:15

When love becomes
as natural as breathing,
and justice welcomes all
without reservation,
we will truly know God's
grace.

First Saturday of Advent

But let justice roll down like waters,
and righteousness like an everflowing stream.

Amos 5:24

When we are tempted
to believe that there is only
enough justice to dampen
the tips of our toes –
sweep us off our feet
with your raging
torrent of righteousness.

Second Sunday of Advent

Let everything that breathes praise the Lord!
Praise the Lord!

Psalm 150:6

Let everything
I touch
I see
be an instrument
of your praise!

Second Monday of Advent

O Lord God, forgive, I beg you!
How can Jacob stand?
He is so small!

Amos 7:2b

Take the wind out of our sails,
deflate our puffed up egos,
puncture our pomposity,
till we are small enough
to cradle in your heart.

Second Tuesday of Advent

'Teacher, which commandment in the law is the greatest?' He said to him,
'You shall love the Lord your God with all your heart, and with all your soul,
and with all your mind. This is the greatest and first commandment.'

Matthew 22:36–38

God, enlarge our hearts,
so we become compassionate.

Deepen our souls,
so we may overflow with your grace.

Broaden our minds,
so we discover you in each person.

Fill us with your love,
so we may share it each and every day.

Second Wednesday of Advent

'They love to have the place of honour at banquets and the best seats in the synagogues.'

Matthew 23:6

When we long for
the best seats
in the house,
hand us a ticket for the
last row in the balcony,
where you wait for us.

Second Thursday of Advent

*For God alone my soul waits in silence,
for my hope is from him.*

Psalm 62:5

In the silence
may I find hope.
In hope,
may I find trust.
In trust,
may I find
you.

Second Friday of Advent

In the second year of King Darius, in the sixth month, on the
first day of the month, the word of the Lord came …

Haggai 1:1

In this year,
in this month,
on this day,
may your Word come,
in the way we least
expect.

Second Saturday of Advent

Let the favour of the Lord our God be upon us,
and prosper for us the work of our hands –
O prosper the work of our hands!

Psalm 90:17

Bless us, Lord,
not so we become rich,
but so more can be fed,
sheltered,
graced, loved –
for this is our work!

Third Sunday of Advent

On that day I will raise up
the booth of David that is fallen,
and repair its breaches,
and raise up its ruins,
and rebuild it as in the days of old.

Amos 9:11

From the ruins of our lives,
you create a new community;
from those days
we would rather forget,
you weave your
future.

Third Monday of Advent

As for me, I am poor and needy,
but the Lord takes thought for me.
You are my help and my deliverer;
do not delay, O my God.

Psalm 40:17

Let me remember
those so poor
that no one notices;
those we forget

as soon as we push them
out of our way.

Third Tuesday of Advent

He loves righteousness and justice;
the earth is full of the steadfast love of the Lord.

Psalm 33:5

In this holy season,
may we love righteousness
more than receiving gifts,
justice more than the jingles
in stores.

Third Wednesday of Advent

… And in front of the throne there is something like a sea of glass, like crystal.

Revelation 4:6a

May we cast
all our worries, fears and doubts
into the crystal sea,
so we may be filled
with your holy presence.

Third Thursday of Advent

The cords of death encompassed me;
the torrents of perdition assailed me;
the cords of Sheol entangled me;
the snares of death confronted me.

Psalm 18:4–5

You uncoil the
cords of death
from around us,
so that they become
the swaddling cloths
of your birth.

Third Friday of Advent

For it is as if a man, going on a journey, summoned his slaves
and entrusted his property to them …

Matthew 25:14

May I be as willing
to take risks with others,
as you are with me.

Third Saturday of Advent

*'For I was hungry and you gave me food, I was thirsty and you gave
me something to drink, I was a stranger and you welcomed me, I was
naked and you gave me clothing, I was sick and you took care of me, I
was in prison and you visited me.'*

Matthew 25:35–36

We search for you
among the powerful and wealthy
while you are with
the kingdom's citizens:
the hungry, the naked,
the sick, the imprisoned,
the lost and lonely.

Fourth Sunday of Advent

*Who shall ascend the hill of the Lord?
And who shall stand in his holy place?
Those who have clean hands and pure hearts,
who do not lift up their souls to what is false,
and do not swear deceitfully.*

Psalm 24:3–4

Washing my hands
with your gritty grace,
I turn to follow you
up kingdom's hill.

Fourth Monday of Advent

On that day it shall be said to Jerusalem:
'Do not fear, O Zion;
do not let your hands grow weak.'

Zephaniah 3:16

On this day
(and on all the days to come)
let me say:
'I will not fear.
 I will not fear.'

Fourth Tuesday of Advent

Then Mary said, 'Here am I, the servant of the Lord; let it be
with me according to your word.'

Luke 1:38

Here am I –
show me how
and where
and who
I may serve.

Fourth Wednesday of Advent

Our God comes and does not keep silence.

Psalm 50:3a

God-who-comes,
may we hear your
whoops of peace
above the din of war;
your songs of hope
drowning out
the oppressor's orders;
your carols of love
silencing cries of hate.

Fourth Thursday of Advent

Now I know that the Lord will help his anointed ...

Psalm 20:6a

Anoint our hands,
our hearts,
our feet,
our very lives,
so we may help others.

Fourth Friday of Advent

You show me the path of life.
In your presence there is fullness of joy;
in your right hand are pleasures for evermore.

Psalm 16:11

Being in your presence
is all the joy
I could ever hope for.

Christmas Eve

Tremble, O earth, at the presence of the Lord,
at the presence of the God of Jacob,
who turns the rock into a pool of water,
the flint into a spring of water.

Psalm 114:7–8

In the silence
and in the singing,
in the wonder
and in the trembling,
in the togetherness
and in the solitude,
I wait …

Christmas Day

No one has ever seen God; if we love one another, God lives in us, and his love is perfected in us.

1 John 4:12

In the faces of my family,
in the stranger on the bus,
in the refugee on the corner,
in the neighbour above me,
I see you
swaddled in each one's
love.

Watching, waiting, listening

An Advent liturgy

Call to worship:

Be patient! God is coming to us!
THE ONE WHO TEACHES JOYOUS SONGS TO ALL CREATION
COMES TO OPEN OUR EARS TO LIFE.

Be strong! God is coming to be with us!
THE ONE WHO PAVES A PATH TO BETHLEHEM
WILL WALK WITH US EVERY STEP OF THE WAY.

Do not fear! Here is your God!
WE WORSHIP THE ONE WHO COMES TO SAVE US.

Prayer:

Now, there is a road
where the blind will see
the signposts leading home.

Now, the burning sand of sin
will become an ice rink
for your children.

Now, the voiceless
become the soloists
in the chorus of hallelujahs.

Now that you have built
a holy way to our hearts,
Advent's Creator,
we no longer need
to wander off your paths …

Now, the crippled
will dance with the stars.

Now, your precious crop
of justice and reconciliation,
planted in oppression's desert,
will burst forth in glory.

Now, the pockets of the fat cats
will be turned inside out
so pocket change can loosen
the chains of despair and grief.

Now that you have come,
Advent's Grace,
we no longer need
to put hope on hold ...

Now, those who refuse
to listen to their enemy
will hear your sweet whispers
of peace for all.

Now, those we have offended
will be blessed by
your healing touch.

Now, those who mutter about
the unfairness of it all
will offer all they have
to the poor.

Now that you are incarnate
in our hearts,
Advent's Joy,
we no longer need
to be afraid ...

God in Community, Holy and One,
now we will call ourselves blessed,
as we pray as Jesus taught us ...

Lord's Prayer

Song

Call to reconciliation:

It would be easy to grumble
that the world has kidnapped this holy season,
emptying us of hope and joy.
But we must admit how often we fail
to tell the true story of Christmas
by how we live our lives.

Let us confess our reluctance to be storytellers,
as well as to live out the story.

Prayer of confession:

Ever-present Peace,
you came to save us,
but that is so hard to remember
in this hectic season.
Our impatience for Christmas to arrive
gets in the way of listening to our children
singing in their rooms.

We let the blinking lights blind us
to your quiet presence in a noisy world.

We get so caught up in the stories of violence,
we cannot hear your voice reminding us
not to be afraid.

Gardener of deserts,
as you poured out your mercy on all who have gone before us,
shower us with grace and forgiveness.

Then, our eyes will be opened to all your wonders,
our ears will echo with the anthems of the angels,
and our emptiness will be filled with the life
gifted to us through Jesus Christ,
our Lord and Saviour.

Silence

Assurance of pardon:

Dear ones of God, this is the good news:
God comes to us to bring the healing of hope,
to put the joy of justice into our hearts.
WE NEED WAIT NO LONGER.
WE WILL GO AND TELL EVERYONE
WHAT WE HAVE SEEN AND HEARD!
THANKS BE TO GOD.
AMEN

Prayer of dedication/offering:

Loving God, you bless us with gifts
so that we might do great things with them:
feed the hungry, house the homeless, lift up the fallen,
speak hope to those in bondage.

Bless these gifts, bless our lives,
as we seek to take the good news into our world.
Amen

Bible readings: Isaiah 35:1–10, Matthew 11:2–11, Luke 1:47–55, James 5:7–10

Song

Reflections:

Especially

when we see you
not only in the twinkle
of a woman's eye
as she lets her grandchildren
lick the icing bowl,
but especially in
a homeless mother
looking at hope's
empty shelves;

when we hear you
not only in the carols
of the children
at evensong,
but especially
in the silent sobs
of the father who
has lost his job;

when we feel you
not just in the embrace
of loved ones
at the airport,
but especially
in the palsied,
papery hands
of the lonely widower;

when we know you
not just in the assertive platitudes
of those who have never held a doubt,
but especially
in the shattered heart
of the teenager
whose faith has slipped
through her fingers:

then
we will know
you have come
just as you
promise.

Or:

It would be a lot easier to get on the bandwagon (which starts the journey to Christmas around November 1st). It would be a lot easier to keep everyone happy by singing as many carols as we can until, by Christmas Eve, we are as sick of them as we are of the 24/7 diet of holiday songs on the car radio. It would be a lot easier to fill our calendars with parties, with shopping, with pushing and shoving with others in the stores, with getting up each morning moaning about *all* that needs to be done that day, and falling asleep with visions of to-do lists dancing in our heads …

But our uncomfortable companion called Advent won't let us get away with doing the season easily.

No, we are challenged to *watch*. Not watch our calendars and smartphones making sure we are getting everything and everywhere, but watch for those signs that say God is up to something in our world, in our lives. Not business as usual, but life that sees those who are overlooked, life that notices those camped by the side of the road, life that observes the brokenness around us, and brings healing into those moments.

We are challenged to *wait*. Not wait in long lines, not wait at the post office anxious to get the cards and packages sent off in time, but wait for – well, we may not know right now. It might be the Holy Family dressed like refugees from a country we are told is our enemy. It might be the wise ones who come as those with mental disabilities, bearing the gifts of genuine acceptance, unconditional love and the treasure of their trust.

We are challenged to *listen*. To listen to the hopes and dreams of those the world is convinced has nothing of value to offer. To listen for the songs of the angels, which often come in the challenging questions of adolescents who seek more than platitudes and easy answers. To listen for the soft breath of the Spirit in the ageing parent who sleeps more hours than ever before, as if gathering strength for the next step on the pilgrimage with God …

Watching, waiting, listening: these are the moments Advent offers to us.

Song

Great prayer of thanksgiving:

The God who is coming to us be with you!
AND ALSO WITH YOU!

Lift your hearts to the One who turns barren deserts into seas of grace.
WE LIFT THEM TO GOD,
WHO FILLS OUR LONGINGS FOR PEACE AND HOPE.

Beloved of God, let us lift our praise and thanksgiving to our Lord.
WE COME TO GOD'S TABLE WITH GLAD SONGS OF JOY ON OUR LIPS.

In that first moment of all time,
you crafted creation out of chaos,
ever-surprising God.
Beauty blossomed abundantly
in every corner of your gift,
everlasting joy and goodness
were the playmates you gave to us
as we strolled through your garden.

But we became too nearsighted
to see the grace awaiting us
in your infinite heart.
Hamstrung by arrogance,
we walked the burning sands of sin,
limping down that dusty road
to death's prison.

You sent Isaiah and Miriam,
Hannah and Amos,
to call us home,
but our ears were stuffed
with the world's empty promises.

Then, you asked Jesus
to walk the holy way,
leaving glory to be born
in a stable.

Therefore, with those who have been raised,
and those who long for your coming,
we join the choirs of angels
who forever sing of your glory:

HOLY, HOLY, HOLY ARE YOU,
GOD WHO FILLS THE HUNGRY.
ALL CREATION SEES THE GLORY OF THE LORD.
HOSANNA IN THE HIGHEST!

BLESSED IS THE ONE WHO COMES SAYING,
'BE STRONG; DO NOT FEAR!'

Holy are you, Hope-full Heart,
and all creation calls your child,
our Saviour, Jesus Christ, blessed.
Listening to you weeping
in the night for your lost children,
he set aside eternity's riches to come:
to fill the shallows of our souls
with your grace;
to snatch us away
from those wild beasts called sin and despair;
to pay the ransom
for those kidnapped by death.

And so, as we prepare to celebrate his birth –
as we journey once again the holy ways,
seeking to hear and proclaim
his life, death and resurrection –
we whisper of that mystery we call faith:

CHRIST DIED,
SCATTERING SIN FROM OUR HEARTS' IMAGINATION.

CHRIST WAS RAISED
AS DEATH WAS KNOCKED OFF ITS THRONE.

CHRIST WILL COME AGAIN,
ACCORDING TO THE PROMISE MADE TO OUR ANCESTORS.

May the gift of your Spirit,
Advent's hope and peace,
be poured out on the simple gifts
of the bread and the cup,
and on those who come
simply to find healing and hope.
And when we have been fed
by your surprising grace
and filled with your peace,
may we go forth to the world,
where our weak hands
will become calloused by compassion;
where we will bend
our feeble knees, reaching down
to lift up the fallen;
where we will become fountains of living water
for those parched by the wilderness
of their lives.

Then, when sorrow and sighing
have been chased away from us,
and we gather with all generations
around your Table in heaven,

everlasting joy will be our song,
and gracious hope will be our refrain,
as we sing to you through all eternity,
God in Community, Holy and One.
Amen

Prayers of concern

Communion

Song

Sending:

The God who makes everything whole
sends us forth to bring healing:
TO LISTEN TO THE BROKEN-HEARTED,
TO COMFORT THE GRIEVING.

The Christ who comes to be with us
sends us forth to stand with the oppressed:
TO RELEASE THOSE IMPRISONED BY GUILT,
TO SPEAK HOPE TO THE LONELY.

The Spirit which calls us to faithfulness
sends us forth to proclaim the good news:
THAT TODAY IS GOD'S TIME –
THE DAY WHEN ALL PEOPLE WILL BE BLESSED.
AMEN

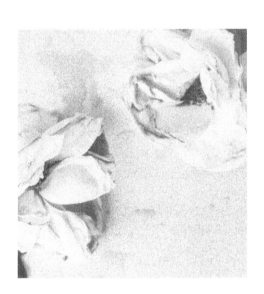

The songs of the angels

A liturgy for Christmas Eve

The soft petals of grace

Bible readings: Psalm 96, Isaiah 9:2–7, Luke 2:1–20, Titus 2:11–14

Greeting:

The people walking in darkness have seen a great light;
on those living in the shadows of death a light has dawned.
JESUS CHRIST IS OUR LIFE AND LIGHT.
IN CHRIST'S NAME, WELCOME!
IN CHRIST'S GRACE, LET US WORSHIP GOD!

Call to worship:

Let us go, just as we are, to see what has happened.
Let us go with the shepherds:
LET US GO AND FIND THE ONE
OF WHOM THE ANGELS SANG.

Let us go with those who are wise:
LET US GO AND FIND THE ONE
WHO BRINGS GOD'S TRUTH TO US.

Let us go with the poor in spirit and in flesh;
let us go with those who are humbled by life:
LET US FIND THE GLORY OF GOD,
BORN IN A STABLE,
AND PLACED IN A FEEDING TROUGH.

Let us go with our friends and family,
let us go with our neighbours and with strangers,
let us go with all the children of God:

LET US GO AND FIND THE ONE WHO COMES
TO LEAD US HOME TO GOD'S KINGDOM.

O come, let us go to the Babe of Bethlehem.
O COME, LET US ADORE HIM! CHRIST OUR LORD!

Christmas prayer:

In the silence of these moments,
whisper of your joy which has come
into the world this night.

In the music and the carols,
sing to us of the grace which fills us this night
and in all the days to come.

In the words we hear,
speak to us of that birth which brings
new life to each and every one of your children.

In the company of friends and families,
of strangers and new acquaintances,
gather us together so we may be your holy family
in this time and place.

In the love and hope which is given to us,
send us forth to tell the good news
to all for whom this is not
the most wonderful time of the year.

God in community, Holy and One,
touch us once again with your wonder,

even as we pray, saying ...

The Lord's Prayer

Carol

Call to reconciliation:

We begin with such great hopes, such big dreams:
we are going to be better;
we are going to treat others more fairly,
love more deeply.
But we come to the manger once again,
knowing our failings
and aware of our brokenness.

Let us confess to the One who comes
so that our lives might be made new.

Prayer for forgiveness:

God who comes to us, forgive us
when our shadowed lives dim your light;
when the tinsel of Christmas means more to us
than your truth;
when our hearts of stone
resist the pain and brokenness around us;
when we care more about what is under the tree
than the damage we do to your creation
and to your children.

Have mercy on us, healing God,
so we might tear down the walls we have built
to keep your love away
and seek your justice for our sisters and brothers.
So our hearts become candles for your son,
our Lord and Saviour, Jesus Christ.

Silence

Assurance of pardon (based on Is 62: 10-12):

Go, go through the city, preparing for the people;
repair, repair all the roads, filling in the holes,
raising a banner for all to see.
God has spoken to all people,
saying to sons and daughters:
'See, your Saviour comes:
to make good on my promises,
to bring redemption to all people.'
AND WE WILL BE CALLED GOD'S BELOVED,
THE REDEEMED OF THE LORD.
GOD WILL SEEK US OUT TO LIVE IN THE NEW JERUSALEM,
WHERE NO ONE IS LEFT BEHIND.
AMEN

Carol

Prayer of dedication/offering:

Remind us,
on this night of celebration,
of the gifts of those who are hungry,
those who are lonely,
those who struggle for hope and joy,
that we might share from our abundance
so that they will be touched by your love and grace,
on this night,
and in all the days to come.
In Jesus' name, we pray.
Amen

Bible readings: Psalm 96, Isaiah 9:2–7, Titus 2:11–14, Luke 2:1–20

Carol

Reflections:

Every year, when the all too familiar story from Luke is read on Christmas Eve on TV, the angel who speaks to the shepherds usually does so with a voice like that of actor James Earl Jones. And the choir? Well, it has to be the Mormon Tabernacle Choir, right? Or something like that.

But this year, finally, I saw and heard the choir as it must have really been on that night in Bethlehem. Residents of the care centre where Teddy my son lives marched in with heads held high, wearing robes that had apparently been found stuffed in a closet somewhere, music folders clutched nervously in their hands. Their voices did not meld perfectly, they tended to wander around trying to find the notes, their words were not clearly enunciated or projected …

But when they started to sing 'Silent night' – the soloist's voice beginning with a tremble and then growing in confidence – that was the moment when Mr Jones' voice left my mind, and that choir which has recorded so many albums sat down with me to listen. For this was the sound the shepherds heard on the hillside – that sent them running down to Bethlehem to find this joy. These were the voices that shattered the complacency of history and forever transformed the hopes of humanity. After all, who better than the most vulnerable to announce that God has chosen to set aside glory and become weak; who better than those the world discounts to tell us of the One who has come to embrace all with God's love; who better than our broken children to sing to us of the Child who will make us – each and every one of us – whole? …

This is the choir, these are the voices I will hear from now on on Christmas Eve, hoping that, when eternity comes, they might let me sing with them.

Or:

The bothy

Every room will be blazing with
light,
so I will have no trouble
finding the place
when I arrive, or so I
imagine;

the table covered in fine lace,
heirloom china
and mirrored silver at each place,
with the feast's aroma
drifting in from the kitchen;

my feather bed will manger
my weary body while
silk sheets swaddle me to sleep
after a relaxing soak
in the jet-streamed tub.

But

what if it is
just a box built out of
river rocks,
the door wind-weathered
and water-buckled,
refusing to stay shut,
as if expecting more folk;
a rough-hewn shelf
in one of the corners
holds a clay pitcher brimming
with cool clear water,
a hand-drawn map to the spring
next to it;
wood has been laid
in the fireplace,
ready to be brought to
life;

a stone bed is all that keeps
one's body from the ground,
just wide and long enough
for a rough blanket,
a candle and matches
where the pillow would be;
and there's a shovel
by the door for taking care
of the necessaries;

it seemed perfect for
you
when you arrived,

didn't it?

Carol

Great prayer of thanksgiving:

On this silent night, God is with you!
GOD IS ALSO WITH YOU!

On this holy night, God's grace comes to us.
OUR HEARTS REJOICE IN HIS BECOMING ONE OF US,
SO WE MIGHT BECOME ONE WITH GOD.

On this Night of nights, the shadows of the world
melt away before God's Light.
WE JOIN THE CHOIRS OF ANGELS SINGING TO THE UNIVERSE
THE GOOD NEWS OF THE BIRTH OF JESUS.

This is the night your heart bursts open with joy,
this is the evening grace pours out of heaven,
this is the moment when you come
to make all things new,
ever-creating God.

You shaped light out of the shadows of chaos,
and moulded your children from the earth,
looking in the mirror as you formed us,
breathing your Spirit into our empty lungs.

Made for life with you
in the garden you designed for us,
we ran away into the wilds of the world,
believing we were wiser than you,
that we could make our own way.
Yet your love never failed us,
your compassion was never taken from us;
you would not abandon us in our foolishness.

You brought us out of slavery
into that land of promise and hope.
You sent your prophets to speak to us
of your disappointment in us,
and to remind us of your dreams for us.
Your love for us was so passionate
that you sent your only Son
to become one of us
that we might be one with you again.

So on this night when heaven reaches down
to caress creation with healing,

we join the angel choirs who sang your glory,
and with your people in every time and place,
carolling the good news which is ours:
GLORIA! GLORIA! IN EXCELSIS DEO!
CREATION JOINS IN THE ANGELIC CHORUS OF JOY.
HOSANNA IN THE HIGHEST!
BLESSED IS THE ONE BORN FOR US THIS NIGHT.
HOSANNA IN THE HIGHEST!

Holiness is who you are, God of Christmas,
and blessings come in Jesus Christ, your Child of Grace.

Finding no warm welcome at his birth,
he knew the cold shoulder of friends at his death;
born in the rude confines of a barn,
he knew the suffering of your children;
sent to be your Word made flesh,
he calls us to follow him into your Kingdom;
proclaimed by the prophet as our Prince of Peace,
he died in the quagmire of human violence.
By his death and resurrection,
you have given new life to all creation.

So, as we gather on this holiest of nights,
we proclaim that mystery we call faith:

BORN IN THE SHADOWS OF NIGHT,
CHRIST IS OUR LIGHT.

DYING ON A ROUGH CROSS,
CHRIST IS OUR LIFE.

RISING FROM A COLD TOMB,
CHRIST IS OUR HOPE.

RETURNING TO US ONCE MORE,
CHRIST IS OUR PROMISE.

Pour out your Spirit upon us,
Wonderful Counsellor,
and on the gifts you have given us.

We lift the broken bread,
praying we would be made whole,
at peace with one another
and reconciled to you.

As we drink from the vineyard of grace,
we believe that our salvation has come,
and we are one with Christ,
our flesh filled with his spirit of sacrifice,
our spirits refreshed by his compassionate heart.

As your joy flows into us,
may we become a river
carrying your justice to the poor;
as your hope sings in our hearts,
may we carry your righteousness to all who suffer.

And as we taste the promise
of the feast you prepare for us in your Kingdom,
may we live for you and serve your children,

as we have been served by the Child of Christmas,
Jesus Christ, our blessed Saviour.
Amen

Prayers of concern

Communion

Carol

Sending:

Go to share the songs of the angels.
WE WILL SHARE THE PEACE AND GOODWILL OF THIS NIGHT
WITH EVERYONE.

Go now to tell of what the shepherds have told.
WE WILL GO TO LISTEN TO THE STORIES
OF THE IGNORED OF OUR TIME.

Go now to be the light of the baby born in Bethlehem.
WE WILL DISPEL THE SHADOWS OF INJUSTICE IN OUR WORLD.

Love came

A liturgy for Christmas Day

Call to worship:

Wonder of wonders – God has come to us!
NOT AS A JUDGE
BUT AS A SAVIOUR.
NOT IN POWER
BUT AS A SERVANT.

Wonder of wonders – God comes to us!
NOT IN EMPTINESS
BUT IN THE WORD MADE FLESH.
NOT IN THE SHADOWS
BUT BRINGING LIGHT.

Wonder of wonders!
GOD IS WITH US!

Prayer:

Angels sang their anthems
at the midnight hour
to awaken a sleeping creation;
shepherds came to worship you –
and went away rejoicing;
wise ones gave their hearts to you,
so they could dwell in yours.
O Emmanuel,
we adore you!

You came to us as a baby:
to hold us in your grace;

you came to us in a stable:
so we would have no trouble finding you;
you came to us in poverty:
to enrich our lives.
O beautiful Messenger of Peace,
we adore you!

You play with us
in the streets of the Kingdom;
you build your home
deep within our souls;
you walk with us
in the winter of life.
O Wisdom from on high,
we adore you!

God in Community, Holy and One,
all the faithful lift their songs of joy to you,
as we pray as Jesus taught us, saying ...

Lord's Prayer

Carol

Call to reconciliation:

God became one of us,
so that we could see the face of love,
hear the voice of peace,
be touched by the hand of grace and

know the heart of mercy.
God comes to us, offering forgiveness and peace ...

Prayer for forgiveness:

You came in weakness, mighty God:
forgive our grasping for power.

You came in humility, Prince of peace:
forgive us for wanting more than others.

You came in poverty, Everlasting One:
forgive us when we do not see your family
sleeping on our streets.

You came in gentleness, wonderful Counsellor:
forgive us for the anger we speak
and the pain we cause.

CHILD OF BETHLEHEM, BE BORN IN US TODAY.
FORGIVE US, HEAL US,
MAKE US NEW:
THEN WE WILL JOIN THE ANGELS
IN SINGING YOUR PRAISES
THIS CHRISTMAS DAY –
AND ALL THE DAYS TO COME.

Silence

Assurance of pardon:

Break forth into singing, children of God:
for the Babe comes to comfort us,
like a mother rocking her son to sleep,
like a father wiping away his daughter's tears.

Carol: 'Joy to the world'

Prayer of dedication/Offering:

As we celebrate the gift which you have shared from your heart,
remind us of those who look for a home,
of those who hope for work,
of those who battle illnesses,
and of all who need the gifts of our hearts
as well as our lives.
In Jesus' name, we pray.
Amen

Bible readings: Psalm 98, Isaiah 52:7–10, John 1:1–14,
Hebrews 1:1–12

Carol

Reflections:

Hope came,
curling up in bed
next to the little
girl
who cries herself
to sleep each night,
while her parents
argue in the
next room;

grace came,
thumbing through the old
magazines,
while sitting silently
in the chair next
to the hospital
bed,
so that when the old
man
awoke, he
would see a familiar
face;

love came,
cracking her back
as she stretched her arms
to the ceiling,
trying to work out
the kinks

from cooking all
night
for the families
sound asleep in
the community centre
hall;

peace came,
taking weapons out
of our hands so
we could build
bridges
and tear down
walls;
you came ...

you
came!

Just as you
promised.

Or:

Late last night, while we were busy wrapping the presents with perfection, busy nicking our knuckles and swearing under our breath, trying to assemble the grandchild's first bicycle, you were neatly hanging glory's garment in the closet, setting out on your journey to us; waiting to be wrapped, not in silver foil with a great big red bow, but in the swaddling clothes of our lives.

And you crept so quietly into our world, coming to keep an eye on all those we overlook; coming to set back on their feet all the ones we knock over in our rush each day; coming to open our hearts to each person we are so determined not to love; coming to make a home for all those we toss aside; coming to keep faith with all who have forgotten how … coming again and again and again and again …

Carol

Great prayer of thanksgiving:

May the Child of Bethlehem be born in you.
AND IN YOUR HEART AS WELL.

Children of God, lift up your hearts.
WE LIFT THEM TO THE ONE WHO CAME TO US
THAT FIRST CHRISTMAS MORNING.

People of God, give thanks to the One who is always with us.
O COME, O COME, EMMANUEL,
TO FEED US AT YOUR TABLE.

When you were weary of chaos
as your companion,
Everlasting God,
you whispered to the Word
who sang creation's song:
mountains sprang to attention,
rivers and oceans splashed your feet,
and the dust from the Carpenter's table
was gathered up and shaped in your image.

Spirit breathed life into us –
that we might dance with you forever.
But when we looked beyond your glory
and saw the decorative temptations
the world dangled before our eyes,
we rushed to embrace sin and death.

Yet you looked past our rebellion,
seeing the people we could become;
and so sent Isaiah and Hannah,
Simeon and Anna as your faithful witnesses.

When we continued to turn up
the world's volume to drown out your pleas,
you sent the Word of Hope
in the silence of a stable.

Therefore, we join with the angels of Bethlehem's skies,
and all those who sing of your steadfast love
in every time and place:

HOLY ARE YOU,
GOD OF CHRIST-FILLED MORNINGS.
ALL CREATION REMEMBERS YOUR STEADFAST LOVE AND FAITHFULNESS,
BREAKING INTO JOYOUS SONG:
HOSANNA IN THE HIGHEST!

BLESSED IS THE ONE WHO BRINGS US THE VICTORY OF GOD.
HOSANNA IN THE HIGHEST!

Holy are you, mighty God,
and blessed is the One who comes in your name,

our Lord and Saviour, your Gift to all the world.
You would not keep the Word to yourself,
but sent him to tell us of your hopes for us.

You did not cling to the Prince of Peace,
but poured him out
to end our enmity and violence with one another.

You could not hold your Heart in your hands,
but allowed him to be broken
on the tree of Calvary,
that we might be made whole forever.

So, as we celebrate his birth, his life,
his death and his resurrection,
we remember the faith which he models for us,
and gives to us as our inheritance:

IN THE BEGINNING, CHRIST WAS WITH YOU,
CREATING LIFE.

ON THE CROSS, CHRIST DIED WITH YOU,
DEFEATING DEATH.

FROM THE EMPTY TOMB, CHRIST ROSE WITH YOU,
BRINGING SALVATION.

FROM GLORY, CHRIST WILL COME AGAIN WITH YOU,
THE LIGHT WHICH COULD NOT BE OVERCOME.

As we gather at your table,
send your Spirit upon the bread and the cup,
and upon us, your children.

As you sent Jesus to be born of Mary,
may we bear the burdens of others;

as you became One with us in the Child,
may we live at peace with all people;

as you have brought us out of the shadows of our sin,
may we carry the Light of the world
to all who live in the darkness of oppression and injustice.

Then, when we gather at your table
prepared for all people in your Kingdom,
we will sing that new song first carolled at creation
and echoed through Bethlehem's hills:
'Glory to God in the highest,
and on earth, peace and goodwill to all.'
Amen

Prayers of concern

Communion

Carol

Sending:

To people who hunger for hope, God sends us.
WE WILL SHARE THE WONDER WHICH HAS BEEN GIVEN TO US.

Into neighbourhoods filled with injustice, Jesus sends us.
WE WILL GO TO STAND WITH THOSE OVERLOOKED BY OUR SOCIETY.

Into a world filled with death and destruction, the Spirit sends us.
WE WILL GO TO BE PEACEMAKERS,
CARRYING THE GIFTS OF RECONCILIATION.

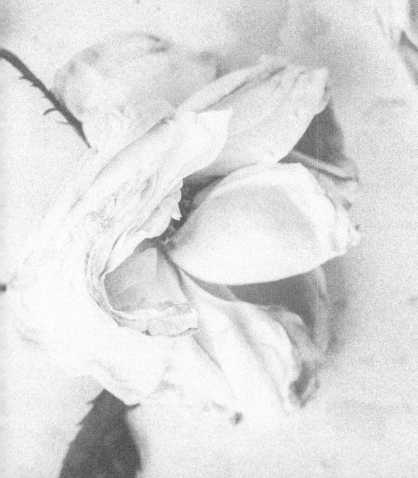

By another road

A liturgy for Epiphany

Call to worship:

We gather wondering,
'Where will we find the Babe
born in Bethlehem?'
WE WILL FIND THE BABE
IN THE LAUGHTER OF CHILDREN,
IN THE WISDOM OF GRANDPARENTS.

We gather asking,
'Where will we find
the Child of Christmas?'
WE WILL FIND THE CHILD
WHERE THE NEEDY ARE GIFTED WITH HOPE,
WHERE THE OPPRESSED ARE SET FREE.

We gather wanting to know,
'Where will we find the Christ,
who has come for us?'
WE WILL FIND OUR HOPE
WHERE FEAR IS OVERWHELMED BY GRACE,
WHERE HATRED IS OVERCOME BY LOVE,
WHERE PEOPLE ARE GRACED BY JOY.

Prayer:

We have heard
of your grace,
Shaper of stars:

from those set free
from injustice;

from our children
who whisper of your joy;
from greeters
of dawn's fresh start;
from late-risers
who listen to the stories
of the needy.

We have heard
of your Light,
Bright Star of the morning:

which can illumine
the shadows of our lives;
which can show
the path to God's heart;
which can point the way
to where we become
servants of the gospel.

We have heard
of your promised peace,
Wisdom's Radiance:

that peace which can end war,
as well as heal our hearts;
that peace which can conquer our fears
and flood us with faith;
that peace which can enter our lives
and overwhelm us with hope.
We have heard of you,
God in Community, Holy and One,

69

and will proclaim your glory to all,
even as we pray, saying …

The Lord's Prayer

Song

Call to reconciliation:

Why do we huddle in the shadowed corners of life
rather than running to the Light of life?
Why do we love the wrong we do
rather than grasping the good news offered to us?
As we struggle with such questions,
let us speak to God of all we have failed to do,
seeking hope and grace as we pray …

Prayer for forgiveness:

We search for your light,
but too often end up settling for the dimness of temptation.
Our motives for seeking Christ are not always pure,
for we expect him to fulfil our desires,
rather than your hopes for us.
We want the gifts of wealth, health, success, fulfilment,
rather than those of servanthood, compassion and peace.
Forgive us, Shaper of our lives,
that we are so foolish as to put our needs ahead of your grace.
Help us to be like those wise people of so long ago:
who found hope, instead of a destination,

who found grace, instead of gratitude,
who found salvation, instead of a sign.

As we journey with your son,
our Lord and Saviour, Jesus Christ,
fill us with the light of your joy and love.

Silence

Assurance of pardon:

Up on your feet!
Grace has been poured into our hearts,
love has flooded our souls,
the light of hope shines in us.
THIS IS THE LIGHT WHICH HAS COME TO ALL,
THE LIGHT WE WILL CARRY AND GIVE TO EVERYONE WE MEET.
THANKS BE TO GOD.
AMEN

Prayer of dedication:

We do not have frankincense or myrrh to offer,
but we *do* have our individual God-given gifts,
and will use them:
so that the lives of the poor might be touched,
so that refugees might be honoured
and so that those searching for meaning
might find a community with us.
In Jesus' name, we pray.
Amen

Bible readings: Psalm 72:1–7, 10–14; Isaiah 60:1–6; Matthew 2:1–12; Ephesians 3:1–12

Song

Reflections:

A friend of mine says that this is the day when a handful of Zoroastrians crashed a Jewish kid's birthday party. Which is a good reminder of how, like the rest of the Christmas story, we have sentimentalised Epiphany, which takes a burden off us and our faith in many ways.

If we dress up these folk with royal robes and sparkly crowns, we can imagine that they were naive, spaced-out stargazers from some mythical country, rather than philosophers and truth-seekers from what is now modern-day Iran. If we focus on the marvellous art that shows the sun shining and all the creatures standing around smiling, we can forget that this birth came in poverty, labour and loneliness, in a stable that hadn't been mucked out in weeks.

We need this sanitised version of this shocking story.

Otherwise, we will have to admit that our way of life is coming to an end, just as it did for the Magi as they returned *'to an alien people clutching their gods'* (T.S. Eliot). Otherwise, we will have to recognise that the birth of this baby means the death of all the old ways of thinking. God is no longer 'out there' only accessible to a privileged class, but walked and talked among us, played and ended up with skinned knees, knew hunger and grief and rejection and even our death. Otherwise, we will have to accept that this is not a story about a sweet, cuddly baby, but about a prodder, a disturber – someone who turns *the whole world* upside down.

We are told at the end of this story that the three visitors went home *'by another road'*. I wonder if that might happen for us too.

Or:

I wonder …

as she cleaned up
the barn,
packing for the trip to
God only knows where,
was Mary muttering
under her breath,
'Men!
They couldn't have
brought diapers,
or given us
a crib?!'

As he pulled
and begged the donkey
to stand still while
the bags were loaded on,
did Joseph think,
'Wise?
They couldn't figure out
I might have used
a new power drill,
or at least some
of that Persian hardwood
that is rarely in the store?!'

The soft petals of grace

When we reach out
to gift those in need,
are we wise enough
to provide what
they really need:
a job,
childcare,
a clinic,
a friend?

I wonder …

Song

Great prayer of thanksgiving:

People of Advent, may the Lord be with you.
AND ALSO WITH YOU!

People of Christmas, lift up your hearts.
WE LIFT OUR HEARTS, OVERWHELMED WITH GRACE,
TO THE ONE WHO WAS BORN FOR US.

People of the Star, offer your songs of joy and thanksgiving to God.
WE WILL SING OUR PRAISES TO THE ONE
WHO HAS REVEALED GLORY AND HOPE
IN THE BABE OF BETHLEHEM.

Radiant God,
in that first moment,
you spoke,

and the light of creation
dispelled the thick darkness of chaos.

You whispered,
and your glory filled the skies.

You sang,
and the dust of the earth
was shaped into your image,
as you breathed life into us.

We could have lived
in grace and peace with you,
for as long as the sun endures,
for as long as the moon hangs in the night sky.
But we were tempted
by the sweet taste of sin,
and overwhelmed with temptation's
wealth of cheap gifts and thrills.

The prophets were sent
to tell of your gifts of joy and peace,
but we listened to the world's news
of success, power, achievement.

Finally, in that dark time of despair,
you sent Jesus,
your servant of salvation.

Therefore, we will join our voices,
with the wise ones, as well as the foolish,
with those of every time and place,

who forever sing of your grace:

HOLY, HOLY, HOLY, GOD OF BRIGHT DAWNS!
ALL CREATION GIVES TRIBUTES OF PRAISE TO YOU.
HOSANNA IN THE HIGHEST!
BLESSED IS THE ONE WHO SAVES THE LIVES OF THE NEEDY.
HOSANNA IN THE HIGHEST!

Holy are you, God of redemption,
and blessed is Jesus Christ, our Saviour.
Overwhelmed with compassion,
he left the glory of heaven
to become a prisoner of sin,
so we could be set free.

Overwhelmed with hope,
he entered death's house,
to break its dark power forever.

Overwhelmed with love,
he travelled another road,
walking to Calvary,
so we might run with joy
into your waiting arms.

So, as we remember his birth,
as we prepare to journey with him this year,
we speak of that mystery called faith,
which is revealed to us through Christ:

CHRIST CAME, THE MORNING STAR OF LOVE.
CHRIST DIED, THE NIGHT STAR OF SALVATION.
CHRIST WAS RAISED, THE RADIANT STAR OF RESURRECTION.
CHRIST WILL COME, THE CONSTELLATION OF HOPE.

Holy One of stars and sinners,
send down your Spirit of hope
upon those gathered around this table,
and on the gifts of the bread and the cup,
that they might make us
your faithful and loving children.

Feed us with the bread of hope,
so when we leave,
we will travel by another road:
to defend the weak,
to speak for the voiceless,
to assist those cast aside.

Refresh us with the sweet nectar of grace,
so we – overwhelmed with joy –
go forth
to enter the houses
of the strangers in our midst;
to enter the despair
of the lonely and forgotten;
to enter the hearts
of everyone we meet.

And when eternity's time begins
and we are gathered around your Table –
with friends and family we loved,
with those we ignored and mistreated,
with all our sisters and brothers of grace –
we will lift our songs of glad joy to you,
God in Community, Holy and One.
Amen

Prayers of concern

Communion

Song

Sending:

Let us go to share the good news of the Babe born in Bethlehem.
WE WILL BRING JOY TO ALL THE CHILDREN AROUND US.
WE WILL OFFER STRENGTH AND HOPE TO THEIR PARENTS.

Let us go to serve the sisters and brothers of this tiny child.
WE WILL GO TO GIFT THE NEEDY WITH HOPE.
WE WILL BRING JUSTICE TO THE OPPRESSED.

Let us go so we may show the way for all who are following the star.
WE WILL SHOW THE PATH TO GRACE AND LOVE.
WE WILL WALK HAND IN HAND WITH ALL WHO SEARCH FOR NEW LIFE.

Lenten and Easter nudges

A daily discipline of Bible readings and short prayers

Introduction

No Damascus road, no mountaintop experience (even on Dun I on Iona), no dreams in the middle of the night, no angels tapping me on the shoulder. No, God seems to get my attention through nudges – those little hints, whispers, giggles, questions, doubts that come my way along each day of my journey. Especially when I stick to a discipline of daily scripture readings, then a word, a phrase, an image appears and – aha! – I find myself on holy ground.

This is a series of responses to those Lenten nudges I have felt over the years of trying to pay attention. I hope they help you on this journey we share.

– Thom Shuman

Ash Wednesday

Psalm 51:1–2

As you lift us out of the tub,
rub the ashes of your dreams
all over us
until we glow with grace.

1st Thursday of Lent

John 1:29

Come upon us,
Spirit of the Lamb,
that we may carry the pains

of the world as far as
necessary.

1st Friday of Lent

John 1:37–39

Walk among us,
grace of God,
teaching us the ABCs
of the Kingdom.

1st Saturday of Lent

Deuteronomy 7:17–19

Open our eyes
to your wonders around us,
so we might
journey unafraid.

1st Sunday of Lent

Jeremiah 9:23–24

Let us boast that we know you as
Love unending,
Peace of justice,
Creation's righteousness,
living out your names in us.

1st Monday of Lent

Deuteronomy 8:11–14

May the wealth
in our pockets
not create scarcity
in our hearts.

1st Tuesday of Lent

Psalm 25:4–5

More than this moment,
a month,
even years –
but all our days (however many)
may we wait – for you.

1st Wednesday of Lent

Psalm 27:4–5

While we play hide-and-seek
(hoping you will not find us?)
you come, searching for us,
to cover us with your love.

SECOND WEEK OF LENT

2nd Thursday of Lent

John 3:16

You came to save the whole world –
but does that really include
me?

2nd Friday of Lent

John 3:28–30

Make us content with a minor role:
ring-bearer, flower girl,
maid of honour, best mate
at the wedding.

2nd Saturday of Lent

Deuteronomy 11:18–21

On the front door of my heart
and the gates of my soul
write grace
so it might be abundant
all my days.

2nd Sunday of Lent

Jeremiah 1:9

Put your words
in my mouth so
others my hear
the grace, the hope, the love
they need.

2nd Monday of Lent

Psalm 145:16

Open your
hand
and fill all the empty spaces
of our souls.

2nd Tuesday of Lent

John 4:48

May your signs
of wonder
be known in the
ordinariness
of our lives.

2nd Wednesday of Lent

John 5:2–6

Is faith
something I believe
because I see
or am I able to
see
because I believe?

THIRD WEEK OF LENT

3rd Thursday of Lent

Psalm 102:18–21

You looked
you heard
you set us free
so may we hear those
who look to us for
good news.

3rd Friday of Lent

Jeremiah 5:1

Though it may only be me
I will cry out for justice,

I will seek truth,
I will serve the poor,
today.

3rd Saturday of Lent

Romans 3:27–28

Tempted to boast,
may I sing a simple song
of grace.

3rd Sunday of Lent

Psalm 42:5–6

My soul settles deep
within me,
so I can hear the song
you are
singing to me.

3rd Monday of Lent

Jeremiah 7:5–7

Feed me with your
words, so I
may always choose
the good.

3rd Tuesday of Lent

Psalm 34:5–6

You love us,
and deliver us, so
we may hear those
in trouble
and serve them.

3rd Wednesday of Lent

John 8:12

Light of the world,
walk among us,
illuminating God
in our midst.

FOURTH WEEK OF LENT

4th Thursday of Lent

John 8:28–30

On our journey,
do not leave us
alone, but be at
our side on every step.

4th Friday of Lent

Romans 6:3–4

Baptised with you,
united with you,
may we walk with you
to the resurrection.

4th Saturday of Lent

Psalm 143:10

May your Spirit
of goodness
be our guide
this day.

4th Sunday of Lent

Mark 8:15

Let the yeast
of your justice
cause us to rise and
serve the outcast.

4th Monday of Lent

John 6:9–12

May our humble gifts
become the feast of
hope
for all who hunger.

4th Tuesday of Lent

John 6:16–20

Come to us,
Water-walker, as we
sail the unruly seas
of our lives.

4th Wednesday of Lent

Jeremiah 18:3–4

Rework us this day
into your clay pots
filled with grace to be emptied
for others.

FIFTH WEEK OF LENT

5th Thursday of Lent

Romans 8:24–25

Fill us with patience,
as we wait for your
hope, just around the
corner of our faith.

5th Friday of Lent

Romans 8:38–39

May nothing –
no thing, no idea,
no person, no fear,
no doubt, no failing –
ever separate us from
you!

5th Saturday of Lent

John 6:67–69

As you come to us
with words of life,
let us go with you
towards death.

5th Sunday of Lent

1 Corinthians 9:19

Though free,
may we willingly choose
to serve your
people.

5th Monday of Lent

Psalm 119:76

Keep your promise
and cradle us in your
steadfast love.

5th Tuesday of Lent

Psalm 91:3

Save us from the
world's traps
and the epidemic
of our fears.

5th Wednesday of Lent

John 10:9

Let us not try
to shut and latch
the gate you leave open,
Good Shepherd.

SIXTH WEEK OF LENT

6th Thursday of Lent

John 10:24–25

Do not keep
us in the dark
but illuminate the way
with your Word.

6th Friday of Lent

John 12:3

Anoint us with the
costly perfume
of your tears shed
over our lives.

6th Saturday of Lent

Jeremiah 31:27

In the coming days,
as you draw nearer
to Jerusalem,
may we draw closer
to you.

HOLY WEEK

Passion/Palm Sunday

Matthew 21:14–17

Palm-wavers or
passionate doubters,
may we not leave you
this week.

Holy Monday

Philippians 3:7–11

Let us toss aside
everything
we think means so much,
so we might be filled
as you empty yourself
for us.

Holy Tuesday

John 12:23–26

Now that your hour
is coming,
may we follow
so we may serve you.

Holy Wednesday

John 12:35–36

Light of the world,
let us walk with you
through the valley
of shadows.

Holy Thursday

John 13:5–8

In the living water
poured into the basin
of your heart,
may we be baptised
into your death.

Holy Friday

John 19:30

In the silence
may we hear your
cry of abandonment;
in the shattering of your soul
may our brokenness
be healed.

Holy Saturday

Job 19:23–27b

As we sing
the blues
on this day,
may we find you
at the piano,
picking out the
tune
we never expected.

Easter Sunday

Luke 24:30–31

Give us new eyes
to see you
in the stranger,

give us new ears
to hear you
in the songs of children,

give us new hearts
to serve you
in everyone around us …

Ash Wednesday

Imposition of ashes and Communion

Silent prayer in preparation for worship:

Take a few moments to bring yourself before God: your present state of mind and preoccupations, as well as your desire to meet God during this time.

Call to worship:

God's people have been called to gather.
FROM AGED GRANDPARENTS
TO BREAST-FEEDING INFANTS,
ALL ARE WELCOME.

God's people have been called to repent.
FROM THOSE WHO WEAR THEIR FAULTS ON THEIR SLEEVES,
TO THOSE WHOSE SECRET HEARTS ARE BROKEN,
ALL ARE WELCOME.

God's people have been called to be reconciled to God.
FROM THOSE WHO HAVE TURNED AWAY,
TO THOSE WHOSE PAIN WHISPERS IN THE NIGHT,
ALL ARE WELCOME.

Song: 'Wait for the Lord' (Taizé)

Prayer:

God of holiness,
your day comes near,
and we tremble,
not out of fear

but from awe and gratitude.
For on your day,
we are fully known,
completely restored,
reconciled to you forever.

Jesus Christ,
Grace-bearer,
as we come to your fast,
may we be filled with your hope;
as we receive your gifts,
may our hearts be opened to others;
as we begin our journey with you,
may we put no roadblocks
on the path to Jerusalem.

Holy Spirit,
Creator of clean hearts,
like water rushes
into an empty hole,
may your sacramental silence
fill the emptiness of our souls.

God in Community, Holy and One,
our treasure, our hope, our joy,
hear us as we pray, as Jesus taught us, saying ...

Lord's Prayer

Song: 'In the Lord, I'll be ever thankful' (Taizé)

Bible readings:

(Choose one or more or all of these Bible readings. You might like to add a chant between the readings to give folk space for reflection (e.g. 'In the Lord, I'll ever be thankful'; 'In our darkness'; 'In God alone'; 'Our eyes are on the Lord', from Taizé)

Joel 2:1–2, 12–17
Psalm 51
2 Corinthians 5:20b–6:10
Matthew 6:1–6, 16–21

Silence (5-10 minutes)

Invitation to Lenten disciplines:

Beloved in Christ,
at the time of the Christian Passover
we celebrate our deliverance from sin and death
through the death and resurrection
of our Lord Jesus Christ.

Lent is the season of preparation
for this great celebration,
the means by which we renew our life
in the paschal mystery.

We begin our Lenten journey
by acknowledging our need for repentance,
for in penitence,
we name those things

which damage us and others
for what they really are,
and we open ourselves
to the One whose love knows no boundaries
and whose mercy is demonstrated to us
in the life of Jesus Christ.

By taking an honest look at our lives,
and repenting of our foolishness;
by praying quietly
but with full hearts;
by letting go of those things that harm us
and by taking on works of love for others;
by reading and feasting on God's Word,
we observe a holy Lent,
and prepare ourselves for the passion
of Holy Week
and the joy of Easter.

Let us prepare ourselves
to come to our God.

Song: 'O Lord, hear my prayer' (Taizé)

Call to reconciliation/prayer of confession:

God begs us to turn from those words, those acts, those obstacles which keep us from being God's people. As we begin our Lenten journey, I invite you to join me, with words and in silence, as we bring our brokenness to God, who desires to make us whole:

APPROACHING GOD,
FOR TOO LONG WE HAVE TRAVELLED OUR OWN WAYS.
FOR TOO LONG WE HAVE SOUGHT TO SATISFY OUR HIDDEN DESIRES.

WE HAVE TRUSTED THE FALSEHOODS OF THE WORLD,
AND RELIED ON THAT POWER WHICH WOULD CONSUME OUR SOULS.

WE HAVE SOUGHT HEALING OFFERED BY IMPOSTORS,
AND REJECTED THE ONE WHO WAS BROKEN FOR OUR WHOLENESS.

HAVE MERCY ON US, GOD,
WHOSE LOVE OVERFLOWS OUR DEEPEST HOPES.

LET OUR HEARTS BE A SANCTUARY FOR YOUR SPIRIT.
LET OUR LIVES ABOUND IN SERVICE TO OTHERS.
LET OUR SPIRITS REFLECT THE ONE WE CALL OUR LORD AND SAVIOUR,
JESUS CHRIST.
AMEN

Silence

Assurance of pardon:

God lets go of the punishment we deserve and gives us mercy in its place. Willingly, God puts a new spirit into us: the spirit of hope and joy.

WE WILL SING TO THE ONE WHO HAS DELIVERED US FROM OUR SINS.
WE WILL PRAISE GOD WITH CLEANSED HEARTS.
THANKS BE TO GOD.
AMEN

The imposition of ashes:

Our ancestors in the faith
used ashes as a sign of repentance,
a symbol of the uncertainty and fragility
of human life.

Like them,
we have tasted the ashes of hopelessness;
we have walked through the ashes
of our loss and pain;
we have stood knee-deep
in the ashes of our brokenness.

God of our lives,
out of the dust of creation
you have formed us and given us life.
May these ashes not only be a sign
of our repentance and death,
but be a reminder that by your gift of grace
in Jesus Christ, our Redeemer,
we are granted life forever with you.
Amen

(Those who wish to do so, may come forward to have the sign of the cross placed on their forehead or hand.)

Silence

25

Responsive invitation to the Table (Is 58):

We try, God knows, we try.
We show up at church, hoping God will notice.
We study scripture, pretending God is reading aloud to us;
we put on those masks to show everyone
how proper we are:
how law-abiding,
how religious;
and we wonder – does God even care?

NOT WHEN WE CLENCH OUR FISTS IN ANGER,
RATHER THAN OPENING THEM IN LOVE.

NOT WHEN WE WORK PEOPLE TOO HARD,
AND PAY THEM TOO LITTLE.

NOT WHEN WE SPEAK BITTER AND HARMFUL WORDS
TO THOSE WE ARE GIVEN TO LOVE.

So tonight, as we begin our Lenten fast,
God offers us a feast. Why?:

So that the broken bread will strengthen us:
to break the chains of injustice,
to take the burden of poverty off our neighbours,
to fix a meal for the hungry.

GOD OFFERS US A FEAST
SO THAT THE CUP OF GRACE WILL FREE US
TO TAKE COATS OUT OF OUR CLOSETS
AND WRAP THEM AROUND SHIVERING SHOULDERS.

TO OFFER SHELTER TO THE HOMELESS
WITHOUT JUDGING THEM.

TO SPEND MORE TIME WITH OUR FAMILIES
AND LESS ON THE INTERNET.

So, come to this table and eat.
Then, you will see the light God offers to your darkness;
then, you will find the path God calls you to walk;
then, you will discover God waiting to help you,
even before you say a word.

WE WILL COME TO THIS TABLE AND FEAST.

Great prayer of thanksgiving:

People of God, the Lord be with you.
AND ALSO WITH YOU.

People of dust, lift up your hearts to God.
WE LIFT THEM UP TO THE ONE WHO CREATED US.

People of ashes, give thanks to the Lord our God.
PRAISE AND THANKS ARE OFFERED TO THE ONE
WHO RESTORES US TO LIFE.

Holy God of creation,
now is the right time to praise you;
now is the moment to sing your praises.
You formed us to live in joy
and peace with you,
but we tore your heart

when we chose our desires
over your dreams for us.
We prefer to splash in sin's mud puddles
than to be cleansed in your living waters.
We hunger more for the adulation of others
than for the quiet intimacy of your grace.
Yet you did not turn away from us
but remained true to your covenant,
calling us to return in words
trumpeted by the prophets;
inviting us to gather in your Kingdom,
entreating us to accept your overflowing love.

Therefore, we glorify you,
joining our voices with those
who had wandered far from you,
but who were brought home;
and with those who seek you now,
in this time and place:

Song: 'Bless the Lord' (Taizé)

Holy are you, Steadfast Love,
and blessed is Jesus Christ, Bread of Life.
Considered a pretender to David's throne,
he is your heart's true Son.
Taking on the poverty of the human spirit,
he shared the abundance of your heart;
weeping over our broken relationships,

he reconciles us with your saving joy;
having nothing he could call his own,
he gives us more than we ever need;
dying like a common criminal,
he gives us life,
releasing us from the grip of sin and death.

Preparing to journey with him once again,
we remember the mystery
of his faithful obedience to your heart:

Song: 'Jesus Christ, Bread of Life' (Taizé)

Holy Spirit,
Heart of Compassion:
like the ashes of our humanity
are placed upon your baptismal seal,
so the brokenness of our lives
is placed on the Table of grace,
so the bread might make us whole,
and the cup might fill us with hope.

Then, in your wisdom,
may we turn to serve others;
in your joy,
may we bear the burdens of others;
in your grace,
may our love overflow to others.

Through Christ, with Christ, in Christ,
in the community of the Holy Spirit,
all glory and honour are yours,
God of holiness, now and forever.
Amen

Communion

While receiving communion, folk are invited to sing 'Eat this bread' (Taizé).

Prayers of concern

Song: 'Jesus, remember me' (Taizé)

Folk depart in silence.

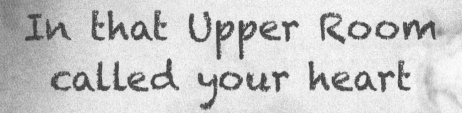

In that Upper Room called your heart

A Communion liturgy for
Maundy Thursday evening

Opening responses:

In remembrance, we gather:
TO BE WITH THE ONE WHO TEACHES US
THE MEANING OF FAITHFULNESS.

In remembrance, we worship:
LIFTING OUR VOICES TO THE ONE
WHO CALLS US TO LOVE ONE ANOTHER.

In remembrance, we feast:
BREAKING THE BREAD WHICH MAKES US WHOLE,
DRINKING THE CUP WHICH FILLS US WITH GRACE.

Evening prayer:

Liberating God,
it was the beginning of hope:
that night long ago when
you prepared to lead
your people to freedom.

As they readied themselves,
you fed them
with your grace,
so that all sin, pain and bitterness
could be set down and left behind
when it was time
to follow you.

Servant Lord,
it was the beginning of salvation:
that night long ago when
you prepared your disciples
for all the things which were to happen.

You humbled yourself by washing their feet,
so they could follow you in service and love
into a world which would reject you
and hang you high on a cross.

Servant's Spirit,
we tell these stories once again
on this night of remembrance.

Here is the bread and wine
which gives us life
and whets our appetite for justice;
here is the basin
which cleanses the stains and wounds
of the world;
here is the towel
with which we will wipe away the tears
of the broken-hearted.

Prepare us for our journey of discipleship,
as we pray as our Servant Jesus Christ
teaches us, saying …

The Lord's Prayer

Song

Call to reconciliation:

How will people recognise us as followers of Jesus?
Simply by how we treat one another.
Let us confess our failure to love as Christ loves.

Prayer of forgiveness:

Creator and loving God,
you kneel to wash our feet,
YET WE ARE RELUCTANT FOR YOU TO SEE THE WOUNDS AND SCRAPES
OF ALL THE PLACES WE HAVE RUN TO
IN OUR ATTEMPTS TO ESCAPE YOU.

You would bathe us in the warm, living waters of your love,
YET WE SPLASH AND PLAY IN THE PUDDLES OF TEMPTATION.

We have received all the gifts you have to offer,
YET WE ARE TEMPTED TO KEEP THEM ALL FOR OURSELVES
RATHER THAN SHARE THEM.

Forgive us, Holy One,
and have mercy on us …

God, what can we give you
for all your wonderful graciousness towards us:

AS YOU HAVE BROKEN YOUR HEART FOR US,
MAY WE OPEN OURS TO SERVE OTHERS.

AS YOU HAVE GIVEN YOUR LIFE FOR US,
MAY WE OFFER OURS TO BRING HEALING TO THE WORLD.
AS YOU HAVE CALLED US TOGETHER AROUND YOUR TABLE,
MAY WE GO FORTH TO FEED A WORLD HUNGRY,
NOT ONLY FOR FOOD,
BUT FOR THAT SPIRIT WHICH BRINGS PEACE AND RECONCILIATION.

THIS WE PRAY AS SERVANTS OF JESUS CHRIST,
WHO CAME TO SERVE US
IN LIFE, IN DEATH AND IN RESURRECTION HOPE.

Time of silence

Assurance of pardon:

On this holiest of nights,
we have received the Good News:

God has come in Christ Jesus to fill us with hope and peace,
to bathe us in grace and mercy.
IN REMEMBRANCE, WE GO FORTH:
TO BRING HOPE WHERE DESPAIR HAS TAKEN UP RESIDENCE.
TO BE SERVANTS TO THOSE WHO ARE BROKEN.
TO LOVE AS SELFLESSLY AS WE ARE LOVED BY JESUS CHRIST,
OUR LORD AND SAVIOUR.
AMEN

Sung response

The soft petals of grace

Bible readings: Exodus 12:1–14; Psalm 116:1–2,12–19; John 13:1–17, 31b–35; 1 Corinthians 11:23–26

Song

Meditation/reflection:

In those early days
when no one was around to watch,
you planted the seeds
which would blossom
into sheaves of wheat;
you began to train
grapevines
to curl round
your fingers
so that,
on that last night,
you could take that loaf of
12-grace bread,
breaking it
into a piece of healing
which could
take our shattered lives
and put us back together
as your beloved;
so that,
in that room,
you could take the grapes

of wrath, fear, doubt,
squeezing them through
your breaking heart,
pouring the sweet nectar
of hope, wonder and peace
into such a simple cup
we cannot begin
to understand
the rich complexity
of your love
but only
taste
on this
night.

Or:

What would you do for a friend, for someone who is dear to you? …

If they were coming home after a hospital stay, you would probably prepare a meal or two for them; maybe go over to their place before they got there, and stick the food in the fridge and post a note: 'Hope you can use this. Welcome home!' You would do that for a friend, wouldn't you? Of course.

What about if they were recovering from a fall, hobbling around on crutches or confined to a wheelchair for weeks or months? What would you do for them? If you were a good enough friend, you would probably run errands for them. If you were a better friend, you would go over and sit with them, watch a show with them, do their laundry, bring in the post. If you were the best sort of friend, you would even be willing to clean their house, even their bathroom, wouldn't you? Of course you would. That's what friends do for one another.

What about if they were diagnosed with cancer and faced multiple treatments of either chemotherapy or radiation or both? They don't have anyone else who can take them, but you have some time to do it. You would drive your friend to hospital and sit in the waiting room while the treatments took place, and maybe even pray for them, and with them, wouldn't you? Of course you would.

Now, would you go to that friend, even that best friend from childhood, and kneel down in front of them, and remove their shoes and socks, and lovingly wash their feet with warm, soapy water and gently dry them off with a towel?

Would you let that friend, even the friend whose heart beats with the same rhythm as your own, kneel down in front of you, and remove your shoes and socks, and lovingly wash your feet with warm, soapy water and then gently dry them off with a towel?

Would you? …

The offering of the gifts

Sung response

Invitation to the table

Song

Great prayer of thanksgiving:

May the God of Last Suppers be with you.
AND ALSO WITH YOU.

Open your hearts to God this night.
WE OPEN THEM TO THE ONE WHOSE HEART IS BROKEN THIS NIGHT.

In the midst of uncertainty and fears, we will praise God.
OUR THANKS ARE OFFERED TO THE ONE
WHO WALKS AND WAITS FOR US
THROUGH LONG NIGHTS.

Creator of the heavens and earth,
when the hour had come,
you lifted up the cup of creation,
pouring it into the emptiness of chaos.
Rivers played tag through the valleys,
stars spangled the blue-black night,
joy danced in the fields of grace.

Given that fountain flowing with living water,
we drank from betrayal's bitter cup;
offered the feast of faith,
we sat down at sin's groaning table.
You asked the prophets to remind us of promises made,
but we continued to embrace the pangs of hopelessness.

Then, because we are your own, you sent Jesus
to glorify you by saving us from ourselves.
Therefore, with those whose feet are covered with sin,

and those whose hearts are gripped by fear,
we join the choirs of every time and place,
forever singing your praises:

HOLY, HOLY, HOLY ARE YOU,
GOD OF TOWELS AND BASINS.
WE JOIN HEAVEN AND EARTH IN PRAISING YOUR NAME.
HOSANNA IN THE HIGHEST!
BLESSED IS THE ONE WHO BECAME A SERVANT FOR US.
HOSANNA IN THE HIGHEST!

Holy are you, God of redemption,
and blessed is Jesus Christ, our Servant, our Saviour.
When the hour had come, he got up from grace's side,
took off his glory, tied humanity around his heart
to cleanse us of our sins.
In the midst of his friends, in the congregation of his enemies,
he kept the promises made to you: to love us to the very end.
Our friend, he welcomed all;
our teacher, he modelled the life of obedience and faith;
our Lord, he endured the snares of death,
that we might have life with you.

Every time we eat the bread, our brokenness is made whole;
every time we drink from the cup, we receive unceasing grace;
every time we come to the table,
we remember that mystery called faith:

IN REMEMBRANCE, WE MOURN CHRIST'S DEATH.
IN REMEMBRANCE, WE LOOK TO THE DAY OF RESURRECTION.
IN REMEMBRANCE, WE AWAIT HIS RETURN.

Now that the hour is come,
send your Spirit upon the gifts of the bread and the cup.
As you cradle the bread in your gentleness,
break it, give it to us, feed us with your compassion
that we might be made whole
and, in our healing,
become servants to a shattered world.
As you take the cup,
mingle its juices with your tears of hope,
so we might carry this gift
to all who have lost everything.

And when there are no more hours to come,
when there is only eternal peace and life with you,
we will gather in that upper room called your heart,
serving our families and friends with grace,
receiving forgiveness from our enemies,
singing your joy forever and ever,
God in community, Holy and One.
Amen

Prayers of concern

Communion

Closing song

The last 24 hours

A vigil for Good Friday

Some believe that the Passion story in Mark's Gospel was written as an Easter vigil for early Christians, to enable them to 'relive' the last 24 hours of our Lord's life, and to prepare to celebrate his resurrection.

In the following vigil, Jesus's final 24 hours are concentrated into about an hour.

Folk gather in silence …

Opening words:

Into the shadows of chaos
THE LIGHT OF THE WORLD STEPS.

From the silence of death
THE WORD OF GOD BREAKS FREE.

For the emptiness of our souls
THE BREAD OF THE WORLD IS BROKEN.

6:00–9:00pm Thursday

Eating with friends: Mark 14:17–25

It was at a table
that the story began:
a people longing
for freedom.
A MEAL TO PREPARE THEM
FOR THE JOURNEY
INTO THE WILDERNESS.

It was at a table

that the story was re-told:
a teacher and students
wondering what
the coming hours
would bring.
A MEAL TO PREPARE THEM
FOR THE JOURNEY
INTO DEATH.

It is at the Lord's table
that the story is remembered:
by people struggling
to be faithful.
A MEAL TO PREPARE US
FOR THE JOURNEY
INTO RESURRECTION.

9:00pm–midnight

Running away: Mark 14:26–50

We convince ourselves
that we would not
act as Jesus' friends do in this story,
but lest we forget:
WE ARE THE ONES
WHO SLIP AWAY QUIETLY
WHEN ASKED TO STAND
BESIDE THE POOR AND OPPRESSED.

Lest we forget:

WE ARE THE DENIERS OF JESUS,
WHEN WE TURN OUR BACKS ON THOSE
THE WORLD DOES NOT RECOGNISE.

Lest we forget:
WE ARE THE GREEDY
WHO CLING TO POSSESSIONS WE NEVER USE
WHICH COULD BLESS OTHERS.

Lest we forget:
WE ARE THE COMFORTABLE
WHO CAN SLEEP THROUGH THE CRIES
OF THE EARTH'S HUNGRY CHILDREN.

Lest we forget:
LET US REMEMBER WHO WE ARE,
AND WHO WE CAN BECOME …

Midnight–3:00am Friday

The troublemaker: Mark 14:53–65

ROCK STAR,
POLITICIAN,
PRO ATHLETE:
Of all the people
you could have been,
you chose to become
a servant –
for us.

POWER,

WEALTH,
DIVINITY:
Of all the privileges
you might have grasped,
you chose to take hold
of a cross –
for us.

PARIS,
CANCÚN,
LOS ANGELES:
Of all the roads
you might have taken,
you chose the one
running through Jerusalem –
for us.

OF ALL THE PEOPLE
YOU MIGHT HAVE DIED FOR –
YOU DID.
AMEN

3:00–6:00am Friday

'I do not know him': Mark 14:66–72

Coming upon that
group of asylum seekers
and rough sleepers
clustered on the walk,
we quicken our pace

and cross to the other side
as quickly as we can,
silently putting them
at the bottom
of that list labelled
'Outsiders'.

When the secretary
knocks on our door
to let us know
the single mum needing assistance
is at the front door (again!),
we simply shake our head:
'Tell her sorry but
we have no resources now',
as we turn back
to ordering more stuff
online.

The little girl
stands at the edge
of the doorway, clutching
her scuffed, faded, stuffed toy
in one hand, her favourite book
in the other, hoping
that this night
Dad might have time to put her to bed,
but with an (almost) silent curse,
you wave her away with a
'I told you not

to bother me!'

Of all the ways
we can say
'I do not know him',
we always seem able
to learn more.

6:00–9:00am Friday

The trial: Mark 15:1–24

No one asked him …
not the Chief Priest
or his bought judges,
though fear would
have deafened them;

not the governor,
balancing political options
on his decision;

not the mob:
pockets full of nightmares,
stomachs full of poverty,
voices brimming with bile,
no goodness or mercy
flowing over
their cupped hands;

no one asked him,

but don't you think
Jesus himself
would have said
(maybe even whispered
to himself):
'Give them Barabbas.'

9:00am–noon Friday

Crucified: Mark 15:15–32

Ridiculed by his enemies,
outcast of his kin,
deserted by his friends,
Godforsaken:
THE MORNING STAR OF CREATION
HANGS
COVERED WITH THE GRIT
OF THE SINS OF THE WORLD.

Nailed to the cross,
the Carpenter of Calvary
REPAIRS OUR BROKENNESS
SO WE MIGHT BE
RESTORED TO GOD'S KINGDOM.

Noon–3:00pm Friday

Mark 15:33

Time of silence ...

3:00–6:00pm Friday

From the Cross to the tomb: Mark 15:34–47

Feet that danced
through the streets
of Jerusalem
welcoming the Messiah
NOW SOFTLY PAD
THE BACK ALLEYS
IN SEARCH OF SHADOWS.

Hearts that leapt with joy
at the sight
of David's true son
ARE THROWN OUT
WITH GOLGOTHA'S
GARBAGE.

Hands that wrapped
a newborn son
in bright bands of cloth
NOW SHROUD
HIS BROKEN BODY
AND LAY HIM

GENTLY,
TENDERLY,
SOFTLY
IN DEATH'S MANGER.

Where glad hosannas
rang out
THERE IS NOW
ONLY
THE SILENT, WEEPING
HEART OF GOD.

Folk depart in silence.

Into the heart of God

A liturgy
for Ascension

Welcome

Opening responses:

We gather in this place;
some of us empty, some of us broken:
YEARNING FOR THE HOLY SPIRIT TO FILL US.

Among fellow seekers who have shown us the way, we come:
TRUSTING THAT GOD WILL CONTINUE TO ILLUMINE OUR HEARTS.

We gather round the Table of grace,
longing to be fed by the Bread of life:
THAT GRACED, WE MAY SERVE OTHERS.
THAT HEALED, WE MAY BRING HOPE TO THE WORLD.

Prayer:

Exalted God,
you are the constant lover
who never forsakes us;
you are the mother
who cradles her children;
you are the teacher
patiently repeating your words for us.
We worship you.

Jesus Christ,
in you
we are convinced

God loves us;
through you,
we are formed
into your people;
with you,
we serve those
the world has forgotten.
We follow you.

Holy Spirit,
you are the power
that gives us peace;
you are the wisdom
that reveals the broken
in our midst;
you are the spokesperson
of the voiceless
to whom we are deaf.
We welcome you.

God in Community, Holy and One,
we lift our prayers to you, as Jesus taught us, saying ...

The Lord's Prayer

Song

Call to reconciliation/prayer of confession:

Called to proclaim repentance,
we are reluctant to look at our own failings.
Invited to witness to God's loving forgiveness of sins,
we would rather not speak aloud of our own.
Let us trust in the One who offers us hope and healing,
as we pray together, saying:

GOD MOST HIGH,
YOU CALL US TO PROCLAIM
A GOSPEL WE FIND DIFFICULT TO PRACTISE.
WE WATCH OUR CLOCKS TO MAKE SURE
WE SPEND MORE TIME WITH OURSELVES THAN WITH YOU.
WE ARE HESITANT TO WITNESS TO YOUR POWER FROM ON HIGH,
FEELING UNCERTAIN OF YOUR PRESENCE IN OUR LIVES.

FORGIVE US, GOD OF LIGHT.
FILL US WITH THE HEALING PRESENCE OF YOUR SPIRIT,
THAT WE MAY PROCLAIM YOUR GOOD NEWS
AS WE PARTICIPATE IN THE LIFE AND SUFFERING OF OUR WORLD,
AS DID YOUR SON,
OUR LORD AND SAVIOUR,
JESUS CHRIST.

Silence

Assurance of pardon:

Choosing to set aside judgement,
God gives us justice;
choosing to let go of punishment,
God fills us with peace;
choosing to release anger,
God's steadfast love rests upon us.

FORGIVEN, REDEEMED, RESTORED –
WE TELL EVERYONE,
THROUGH THE LIVES WE LEAD,
WHAT GOD HAS DONE FOR US.
THANKS BE TO GOD.
AMEN

Sung response

Bible readings: Psalm 47, Luke 24:44–53, Acts 1:1–11, Ephesians 1:15–23

Song

Reflection/meditation:

We stand
with our mouths agape,
staring up at the
sky,
wondering,

arguing,
where you have gone,
when
you will come back,
and so,
we keep our hearts
closed tight,
not seeing you
in the child scrounging
through the
garbage;

we shuffle our
feet,
the dust covering
our sin-scuffed
shoes,
thus
unable to see your
footprints
leading us to
your
Kingdom;

certain we have
all the facts,
convinced by the
arguments
of our favourite
commentators,

we shutter our minds,
until you come along,
your voice
singing
glad songs of
praise.

Or:

The Day of Ascension doesn't seem to fare very well in most Churches. In fact, this 'day' doesn't even get a Sunday to itself: it is observed on the Thursday between the 6th and 7th Sundays of Easter. No wonder so many folk, including ministers, don't know much about it.

So why pay attention to the Ascension of Jesus?

In part, because the story is a reminder that the earthly ministry of Jesus has ended: at Pentecost, the torch is passed on to the disciples, and down to us through all the centuries. Now, the story says, it is up to us – we are the ones who are called to be more compassionate, more accepting, more forgiving, more just: more faithful.

The story also confirms what the Resurrection first showed – that Jesus is now the Risen One, the One who sits at the right hand of God, the One who continues to work – with us, through us, despite us – to bring about that new heaven, that new earth, that new hope, that new life which has always been God's intention for all creation.

Because Jesus is at the right hand of God, with authority and power, we can trust that such power will continue to pour out God's grace upon us. The One who became fully human continues to bring our humanity, our brokenness, our possibilities, our hopes and dreams into the heart of God. We are not forgotten by the One who came in a humble birth, and died the death of a common criminal. And God, whose heart broke when Jesus died, who brought him out of the grave, who gave Jesus new life, will also not forget us, but will do the same for his people.

Offering of the gifts

Sung response

Invitation to the Table

Song

Great prayer of thanksgiving:

The Ascended Lord be with you!
AND ALSO WITH YOU!

Lift up your hearts to the One who gives us a spirit of wisdom.
WE OFFER OUR HEARTS TO JESUS, WHO OPENS GOD'S WORDS TO US.

Clap your hands, God's people!
Sing songs of praise to our God!
WE SING PRAISES TO THE ONE WHO BLESSES AND BLESSES US!

We do indeed lift loud songs of joy to you,
Awesome God!
Everything in heaven and on earth

provides all the proof we need of your goodness and mercy.
But closing our hearts to such evidence,
we looked to our own wisdom,
devising foolish ways to save ourselves.

Patiently you waited,
hoping we would return to you,
but when you could no longer wait,
you came to us
in your Word made flesh and blood.

Therefore, with all your people
of every time and every place,
we sing our glad songs to you:

HOLY, HOLY, HOLY LORD GOD,
SOVEREIGN OVER ALL THE EARTH.
THE RICHES OF YOUR GLORIOUS CREATION FOREVER PRAISE YOU.
HOSANNA IN THE HIGHEST!
BLESSED IS THE ONE WHO WILL RETURN FOR US.
HOSANNA IN THE HIGHEST!

All glory is due to you, God on high,
and blessings on your Son,
our Lord and Saviour, Jesus Christ.
Stripping himself of glory, he came
that we might be clothed
in the power of the Holy Spirit.
Wearing the thorny crown of death,
he is the Head of all the Church,
his Body made whole for the world.

As we remember his life, his service,
his death, his resurrection, his Ascension,
we speak of that mystery called faith:

CHRIST DIED TO REVEAL SALVATION TO US.
CHRIST ROSE TO REVEAL RESURRECTION LIFE TO US.
CHRIST ASCENDED AND WILL RETURN TO REVEAL GLORY TO US.

We will not stop giving thanks to you,
generous and wonderful God,
as we pray that you would pour out your Holy Spirit
upon your children gathered at the Table,
and upon the gifts of the bread and the cup.
We are filled with Christ's presence so that we may go
and pour out and give ourselves to others:
telling your story of grace to those who feel hopeless;
carrying your mercy to those who can never forgive themselves;
sharing cups of cold water with those who thirst for peace.

Then, when we gather at your feast in glory,
seated with our sisters and brothers from all time,
we will clap our hands, shouting our joy to you:
God in Community, Holy and One,
now and for evermore.
Amen

Prayers of concern

Communion

Song

Blessing:

We will not cling tightly to the past:
BUT GO FORTH AND SERVE OUR GOD.

We will not spend time looking up to heaven:
BUT GO AND SERVE CHRIST'S BROTHERS AND SISTERS HERE ON EARTH.

We will not hoard our gifts:
BUT SHARE THE SPIRIT WHICH DWELLS IN US.

That's when it happened

A liturgy
for Pentecost

Call to worship:

On this first day, the Lord's Day,
we gather in this place:
THOUGH WE HAVE DIFFERENT GIFTS
WE ARE BLESSED BY THE SAME GOD.

On that great day of Pentecost
the disciples gathered together:
THOUGH UNCERTAIN, THEY TRUSTED IN GOD'S FUTURE.
THOUGH MANY, THEY WERE ONE IN CHRIST.

On the last day of all time,
God's daughters and sons will be together in one place:
UNTIL THEN,
WE WILL TALK OF GOD'S DREAMS,
WITH EVERY BREATH WE TAKE,
IN EVERY MOMENT WE LIVE.

Prayer:

Astonishing Creator,
at Pentecost,
you could have been
calm, cool, analytical –
but you decided to
no longer play it safe,
but once again
(and for all time),
unleashed the Spirit

into our babbling
and humble-jumble lives.

Living water,
like an artist using
a variety of mediums,
you proclaim good news to us:
to those who hunger for hope,
you offer the banquet of justice;
to those parched by loneliness,
you offer the precious cup
overflowing with your tears.

Unbridled Spirit,
you calm us when
we are racing around
like four-year-olds
playing tag;
you come rushing
through our soul's backyard,
knocking our dirty lives
off the clothesline,
to shawl us in
salvation's spring garb.

May our words please you,
God in Community, Holy and One,
as we pray as Jesus taught us …

The Lord's Prayer

Song

Call to reconciliation:

Called to be one body,
we live as fragmented members.
Our selfish desires,
our lust for more,
our belief we have no need of others,
leads not to unity,
but to division.

Let us confess our brokenness
to the God who saves us ...

Prayer for forgiveness:

In the arguments which divide us,
Hope's heart,
we cannot hear your voice calling us to be one.
In the rush to judge others
who speak, dress or look different from us,
we cannot stop to experience your grace.
In our devotion to ourselves and our needs,
we cannot open our hearts to receive your gifts.

Silence our babbling lives,
sculptor of salvation,
so we might hear the clear, sweet
voice of the Spirit
announcing that we are forgiven,

calling us to proclaim the good news
to all the world,
baptising us into the body of Jesus Christ,
our Lord and Saviour.

Silence

Assurance of pardon:

On this day, as on every day, God stands
arms wide open to embrace us,
heart wide open to forgive us.
Friends, this is the good news:
GOD'S GLORY IS FOREVER.
GOD'S GRACE WILL NEVER END.
WE WILL REJOICE IN GOD'S HEALING HOPE,
AS LONG AS WE HAVE BREATH.
AMEN

Prayer of dedication/Offering:

May our gifts join your dance of healing and hope
for those living in despair.
May our voices join the multitude of languages
crying out for justice.
May our hearts embrace those
you are bringing into our community –
on this great day of Pentecost
and in all the days to come.
By the Spirit's grace, we pray.
Amen

Bible readings: Psalm 104:24–34, 35b, John 20:19–23, Acts 2:1–21,
1 Corinthians 12:3b–13

Song

Reflections:

When the Spirit comes,
she will put dancing shoes
on my two left feet,
lace them up
and lead me out
onto the floor,
where we will enter
the Argentine tango
competition;

when the Spirit comes,
she will wander through
the barren garden of my soul
and,
as she opens her hands,
butterflies will skitter
from withered hope
to dashed dreams,
breathing them back
to life;

when the Spirit comes,
and finds me brooding

by the stagnant pool of tears,
she will dive right in,
drenching me with God's joy,
then teach me how
to float on my back
(without sinking),
pointing out the flames
flitting about our heads
like fireflies.

Come,
Spirit,
come …

Or:

Just your typical Sunday morning.

Very nice prelude by the organist; announcements about the Heifer Project luncheon next week, a piano recital this afternoon (including twin sisters from the church), opportunities to join the choir, a Bible study group; good job by the lay liturgist with the opening parts of the service; the typical enthusiastic singing by the congregation. The scripture lessons were read, with time for silence and reflection after each one; the choir shared a superb anthem that connected with the Lord's Supper. The sermon? Well, maybe a B today: talking about the 'tools of the trade' we are given as God's people, and how we might use them (while wearing a tool belt and using some other 'visuals'). After that, I invited folk to remember all the blessings God had given them, and to share from that abundance as we offered our tithes and gifts to God …

That's when it happened.

I glanced at the back and noticed that there was only one usher ready to take up the offering. I figured Bob, being the rather proper person he is (always a coat and tie on Sunday), would simply ask one of the other folk sitting in the back to help, as usually happens. But he went over to Paul, and asked him. I could tell by Paul's reaction that he thought he was being asked to put something in the plate, and Paul has nothing to put in the plate, as Paul is poor and on disability, so Paul simply shook his head 'no'. Then Bob said something else, and Paul got a quizzical look on his face. Bob spoke again, and handed Paul the other offering plate, and together they went up the centre aisle to begin taking up the offering.

Mr Dressed-in-his-Sunday-best and Mr Wearing-whatever-he-could-find-to-put-on-this-morning living out the gospel before our very eyes, the soft petals of grace gently falling on the carpet behind them as they journeyed together down the Main Street of the Kingdom. The Spirit must have thrown some grit in our eyes, for many of us were blinking pretty rapidly. God must have turned up the sun because it seemed just a bit brighter in there, and I could swear I heard Jesus whisper, 'Finally, finally.'

And then we gathered at that Table – where the homeless will offer their brokenness to the owners of McMansions so that all might be healed; where little children will hold their grace-filled sippy cups to the mouths of those with palsied hands; where those who have trouble putting two thoughts together will explain the gospel to professors of philosophy; where the voiceless will have the solo part in the anthem; where the gospel is not just a book on the shelf but Paul, Bob and the rest of us living our lives. Just your typical Sunday morning – now that the Spirit has come!

Song

Great prayer of thanksgiving:

May the Spirit of Pentecost be with you!
AND ALSO WITH YOU!

People of Pentecost, lift up your hearts.
COME, HOLY SPIRIT, AND FILL OUR HEARTS WITH
THE FLAMES OF YOUR JUSTICE FOR OTHERS.

Spirit's Children, join your voices in praise.
COME, HOLY SPIRIT, TO TEACH US NEW SONGS
OF COMPASSION AND SERVICE.

Architect of the universe,
when chaos had grown old and wrinkled,
you sent the Spirit to give it a new face –
imagining, shaping, painting –
until the starlight shimmered
on the watery deeps,
until the earth trembled
from the trees dancing in delight.

You created critters which tiptoe
across our floors at night,
and great whales that play
hide-and-seek with submarines.
You formed humanity in your image,
and filled us with your Spirit
so we could sing praises
to you every moment.

But sin and death
took our breath away
with their fireworks made
of futility and fear,
and we chased after them
clapping our hands in delight.

Prophets came, entreating
your daughters and sons to come home,
but we thought they were drunk
on ecstasy's sweet wine.

So, you sent Jesus,
hoping to get our attention
with glory made flesh.

So, with all who have gone before us,
and all who will come after,
we sing our songs of praise:

HOLY, HOLY, HOLY ARE YOU,
GOD WHO SWEEPS AWAY ALL BARRIERS.
ALL CREATION TREMBLES AS IT REJOICES IN YOU.
HOSANNA IN THE HIGHEST!

BLESSED IS THE ONE WHO BREATHES THE HOLY SPIRIT ON US.
HOSANNA IN THE HIGHEST!

Holy are you, our only hope,
and blessed is Jesus Christ, your Son.

When our souls thirsted
for your presence,
he came,
to offer us a drink of grace.

When our hearts cracked
from the strain of unbelief,
he came,
to mend us with faith.

When we had lost our way,
he came,
to follow agony
to its bitter end,
so we could begin
our journey home to you.

As we remember his life, his death, his rising,
as we celebrate the fulfilment
of the Spirit he promised,
we sing of that mystery we call faith:

CHRIST DIED,
GIVING HIS LAST BREATH FOR US.

CHRIST WAS RAISED,
THE FRESH BREATH OF RESURRECTION FILLING HIM WITH LIFE.

CHRIST WILL COME,
BREATHING NEW LIFE INTO US FOREVER.

Pour out Pentecost's Spirit
upon these gifts of the bread and cup,
and on your daughters and sons
who hunger for your goodness.

As we eat of the Bread,
may grace dance in our hearts
to feed and move us
to rush out with healing
for a broken world.

As we drink from Hope's cup,
may it cascade through us,
filling us with your undying compassion –
till we become lives of flowing love
for a parched people.

And when that great day comes
when you gather your children in one place,
around one great table,
we will receive the Spirit and sing to you,
with one voice, one heart,
God in Community, Holy and One.
Amen

Prayers of concern

Communion

Song

Sending:

God's glory has filled our hearts!
WE WILL GO TO EMPTY OURSELVES FOR OTHERS.

Christ has given himself for us!
WE WILL GO TO OFFER OURSELVES TO EVERYONE IN NEED.

The Spirit gifts us with new life!
WE WILL GO TO BE A BLESSING TO EVERYONE WE MEET.

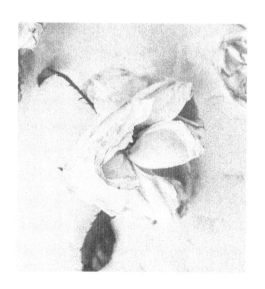

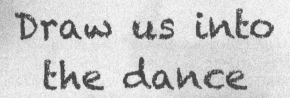

Draw us into
the dance

A liturgy for Trinity Sunday

Call to worship:

Called to be faithful stewards of creation, we come to worship:
TO SING TO THE ONE
WHO HAS CREATED ALL THAT IS GOOD, BEAUTIFUL AND TRUE,
AND WHO HAS SHARED EVERYTHING WITH US.

Called to be disciples of Jesus Christ, we come to learn:
TO FOLLOW THE ONE
WHO MEETS US IN EVERY MOMENT OF OUR LIVES,
IN EVERY PLACE WE FIND OURSELVES.

Called to proclaim the Good News of Easter, we come to find the words:
TO BE TAUGHT BY THE SPIRIT,
WHO MOVES IN AND THROUGH US,
AS WE SERVE THE WORLD.

Prayer:

Hearing your whisper,
creation tingles with anticipation,
knowing that goodness
and wonder are your heart's desires.

Listening to your instructions,
the universe shimmers with delight,
and all creatures fall down
to worship you.

Imaginative God,
you are as close
as the early-morning breeze.

God spoke,
and you ran forth
to sprinkle the heavens
with shimmering stars;
you poured the waters of grace
into the hollows of the earth
so all life might emerge.
Bone of our bone,
flesh of our flesh,
you are as close
as the love which
fills our hearts.

God dreamed,
and you flowed over chaos –
shaping, spinning, weaving
peace, wonder and joy
into the fabric of all life.
Your passion for hope
became flames which
dance in our hearts.
Spirit of fanciful faith,
you are as close
as a butterfly's wings
brushing our cheeks.

The soft petals of grace

You are closer to us
than we ever dared hope,
God in Community, Holy and One,
and so we lift our prayers to you, saying …

The Lord's Prayer

Song

Call to reconciliation:

When God looks at us,
the One who created us sees hope, joy, grace, life.
But all too often,
others see us as we are – broken, hurtful, sinful.
Let us confess our deeds and words to the One who loves us,
and longs to re-create us in the image of true life.

Prayer for forgiveness:

Why do you pay us any attention,
Artist of creation?
Created in your image,
we show faces filled with desire to do good
but offer hearts filled with anger to those around us.

Called to be disciples of Christ,
we all too often are seen chasing after
the false promises of the easy life.

Offered the role of being stewards of creation,
we think that everything you have created
is to be used up
so we can enjoy life,
with no thought about future generations.
Yet you have declared everything you created to be good,
even us, God of unexpected grace.
So we know that,
in Christ Jesus, our Lord and Saviour,
you will reshape our greed into generosity,
our bitterness into blessings,
and our brokenness into lives
poured out in service to our sisters and brothers.

Silence

Assurance of pardon:

Lives that are chaotic become cradles of peace;
hearts malformed by meanness are reshaped into goodness;
souls filled with despair are cleansed with grace.
THIS IS THE GOOD NEWS:
THE GOD WHO CREATED US
IS THE SAME GOD WHO REDEEMS US.

THE GOD WHO REDEEMS US
IS THE GOD WHO SENDS US FORTH TO SERVE.
THANKS BE TO GOD, WE ARE FORGIVEN!
AMEN

Prayer of dedication/Offering:

Use our gifts, Holy Community of Love,
as you reach out to heal the broken,
as you take the hands of the lost
and as you pull out a chair to welcome
the outcast to your table of wonder and hope.
This we pray.
Amen

Bible readings: Genesis 1:1–2:4a, Psalm 8, Matthew 28:16–20, 2
Corinthians 13:11–13

Song

Reflection:

I toss
God
into the air,
watching the divine
spin and sparkle;

next I add
Jesus
to the mix, carefully
throwing each
from one hand
to the

other, confident
I will not drop either
One;

then, pulling the
Spirit
from my back pocket, I begin
that simply
complex
process of keeping all
Three
in the air;

as I settle
into the rhythm
of keeping the
Holy Community
under my control
(propelling them
faster and faster
until they
become a
blur no one can
comprehend),

the audience sits
spellbound
by my theological
dexterity,
and none of us

hear
your gentle whisper,

*'Why do you think
it is all an
act?'*

Or:

There are all sorts of explanations that might be offered when it comes to the doctrine of the Trinity, all sorts of theologians can be quoted, all manner of creeds and confessions might be affirmed. And – after all that – most of us are *still* confused.

One image I find helpful is that of the dance – the Holy Community joining hands and joyfully being in relationship with one another. Sometimes, God is the one who keeps the underlying beat going, Jesus might teach a new step that the others had not thought of yet and the Spirit will improvise the tune so that the tempo and rhythm is not always the same. But they are always in step; they are always focusing on one another, even as each is aware of the particular part they play in the dance.

And they want to share that dance with us, to teach us the steps, to help us hear the music.

The Father reaches out in Love, inviting us to dance, to show us those moves called grace, wonder, laughter, peace. The Son connects with us in Love, taking us by the hand to draw us into the dance, whether we are hurting, or angry, or grieving, or broken, or lost. And the Spirit welcomes us, enfolding us in Love, as we are taught to dance with abandon, with kindness, with hope, with gentleness.

And as we dance, we discover that the Trinity is not so much a doctrine as it is a relationship – with us!

Song

Great prayer of thanksgiving:

May God in Community be with you.
AND WITH YOU AS WELL.

Shaped in the divine image, let us open ourselves to the Creator.
WITH GRACE-FILLED HEARTS, WE COME TO THE REDEEMER'S TABLE.

Called to be God's household, let us offer our praises.
WE REJOICE THAT THE HOLY SPIRIT HAS BROUGHT US,
FROM MANY PLACES, HERE TO OUR HOME.

At the beginning,
God of Imagination,
you finger-painted
sunrises and sunsets
on the blank canvas of chaos.
You sang creation's cantata,
while suns, moons and stars
kept watch over your delights.
You laughed, while
lions, tigers and bears
danced joyfully in the meadows,
and everything that
wiggles, creeps, crawls

clapped their hands in time.
When you would have
clothed us in glory,
we found sin and death
to be a more comfortable fit.

Prophets came teaching obedience
and calling us to faithful lives,
but we continued to insist
on having control of our souls.

So, you sent Jesus,
to make our brokenness
whole once again.

So, with grace, love and unity,
our faithful companions and teachers,
and with all the saints of every time and place,
we lift our songs of thanksgiving:

HOW MAJESTIC IS YOUR NAME IN ALL THE EARTH, HOLY ONE.
ALL CREATION GREETS YOU WITH GLAD SONGS OF PRAISE.
HOSANNA IN THE HIGHEST!

BLESSED IS THE ONE WHO COMES TO MAKE US DISCIPLES.
HOSANNA IN THE HIGHEST!

Holy are you, God over us,
and blessed is Jesus Christ, God-with-us.
He took off glory's garb
to put on humanity;
he set aside heaven's honour

to be crowned with disgrace;
he spoke of love and hope,
silencing our enemy, pride;
he went into the grave
to free us from death's grasp.

As we remember his life, death and resurrection,
as we celebrate his re-creating power in us,
we speak of that mystery called faith:
CHRIST DIED, CROWNED WITH DEATH'S THORNS.
CHRIST WAS RAISED, CROWNED WITH RESURRECTION'S WONDER.
CHRIST WILL COME, TO CROWN US WITH GLORY AND HONOUR.

Send your Spirit to flow over
the gifts of the bread and the cup,
and to bring light and goodness
to those who gather around your table.

As we break the Bread of life,
may we become living hope
to a world mired in despair.

As we drink from the Cup of grace,
may we cradle your kindness and peace
in our hearts and souls,
so we might be poured out
to those who thirst for your
peace and gentleness in their lives.

And when your dreams which began at creation
are realised and all time comes to an end,
when we gather around your table,

with saints and sinners, disciples and deniers,
we will find ourselves closer to you
than we ever thought we might be,
singing your praises forever and ever,
God in Community, Holy and One.
Amen

Prayers of concern

Communion

Song

Sending and benediction:

God, who created you in the divine image, sends you forth:
WE GO:
TO REFLECT THE PRESENCE OF OUR CREATOR
TO EVERYONE WE MEET ALONG THE WAY.

Jesus, who has redeemed you,
has established God's Kingdom in our midst:
WE GO:
TO BRING HEALING AND HOPE
TO ALL THE BROKEN OF THE WORLD.

The Holy Spirit, who calls you to be God's people,
goes with you to many places:
WE GO:
TO TEAR DOWN THE WALLS WHICH DIVIDE US,
AND TO BUILD LIVES OF TRUST IN ALL OF GOD'S CHILDREN.

And now,
may the peace of the rolling waves,
the peace of the silent mountains,
the peace of the singing stars,
and the deep, deep peace of the Prince of Peace,
be with you now and forever.
Amen

Mountaintops, valleys and every place between

A liturgy for Transfiguration Sunday

Meditative music

Opening responses:

From a cloud and in a crowd,
God speaks to us:
CALLING US TO BE LOVERS OF JUSTICE,
TO SHARE HOPE WITH THE BROKEN.

On mountaintops and in neighbourhoods,
Christ calls to us:
WITH A WORD AND WITH WONDER,
MOULDING US INTO WHO WE ARE.

On the playground and at the workstation,
the Spirit whispers in our hearts:
GATHERING UP OUR FEARS AND OUR DREAMS,
AND OFFERING THEM TO GOD.

Prayer:

Listener of our souls,
when we become adept
at chicanery,
you hand us the rule book
on fair play you have written.

When we brag
about all our achievements,
your glory silences our prattling

so we can hear your
soft whispers of wonder.

Listener of our hearts,
when we memorise all
the goals and objectives
taught to us by sin and death,
you become the nemesis
of our mismanaged lives.

When we become so
hardheaded we butt at grace,
you soften our pride with
the warmth of your peace.

Mirror of God's love,
when our lives are veiled
with pride and ignorance,
you turn us inside out
to reveal who we truly are.

When we turn our hearts
this way and that,
thinking that God's glory
resembles some abstract art,
you pull out a snapshot
of Jesus from your purse.

God, with you we never lose heart.

Lord's Prayer

Song

Call to reconciliation:

Sometimes we wait for God
to astound us with whirlwinds of wonders,
while God silently offers us grace.
God waits to forgive us,
so let us hold nothing back,
but place our trust in the One
who listens to our prayers
and answers us with mercy.

Prayer of confession:

Glorious Creator,
we admit that we are afraid to come near you,
scared that if we do,
you will see how our faces darken with anger
as we speak hurtful words,
whiten with fear of those who are different,
redden from the depths of our desires.
God, we can spend so much time gazing in the mirror of our longings,
that we are unable to see the faces etched with loneliness,
hollowed by hunger,
overshadowed by hopelessness.

Holy One, you reveal the mystery of your grace
by pouring out mercy upon us.
As you bend down to listen,
may we speak your love to all those around us.
As you call us into your presence,
you send us out to do your justice,
which brings hope to the world.
This we pray in the name of Jesus Christ,
our Lord, our Saviour,
our love, our justice.

Silence

Assurance of pardon:

On mountaintops and in valleys,
in our hopes and in our hearts,
God knows us better than we know ourselves –
and God forgives us when we cannot forgive ourselves!

BY GOD'S MERCY, WE ARE FORGIVEN.
BY GOD'S MERCY, WE ARE MADE WHOLE.
BY GOD'S MERCY, WE ARE EQUIPPED TO SERVE OTHERS.
THANKS BE TO GOD.
AMEN

Bible readings: Exodus 34:29–35, Psalm 99, Luke 9:28–43, 2
Corinthians 3:12–4:2

Song

Reflection/meditation:

Transfiguration Theme Park

If you build it …

The architect has rendered
her drawings,
the financing is being
lined up –
so that soon at
the Transfiguration Theme Park
one can ride Pete's
roller coaster,
climbing high up into
the mist –
before plummeting straight down
(hands raised high,
stomach clenched,
eyes wide in fear or wonder)
into denial's
chill waters;

Elijah and Moses
tag team at the fortune-telling tent,
their wisdom dispensed
for only five bucks;

at the funhouse,
God stands just behind us,
peering over our shoulders,
roaring at the silly shapes
of our faces
and lives reflected in
the mirrors;

and for a quarter a chance,
one can try to
knock Jesus off
his mountaintop
into the valley below ...

When we come up with
all our grandiose
schemes to market you, God,
silence us
with a look,
so we can
pay attention to
your heart.

Or:

I don't know if the Transfiguration really happened as we are told.
But I believe that the story is in the Gospels for a reason:
that it says something to us about how following Jesus
will transform our lives in unexpected ways;
about how

we are given visions of the Kingdom
in everyday life.

I don't know if God spoke in a voice
which Peter and the others
could clearly understand.
But I do trust that God speaks to us –
if we are willing to open ourselves up:
that the voice of God is heard in the laughter of children,
in the questioning doubts of teenagers
and in the stories of wise ones
who are only too willing to share,
if we'd just stop
and sit down
and listen …

I don't know if what Luke tells us is an actual event, an allegory,
a short story or what.
But I do know that I am called to act on what I believe
and to trust in the story.
Which is,
that in Jesus I catch glimpses of what God is doing in the world –
that in Jesus I see someone I want to follow for the rest of my life;
that with Jesus
I find myself on mountaintops
and in valleys
and in every place in between,
but never find myself alone
anywhere.

But to act, I need to trust
what God is saying:

that the world can be transformed from darkness to light,
even as I can;

that love is stronger than hate;

that I am loved,
even when others tell me differently;
that goodness is the path which I am meant to walk,
and others will help me to follow the Way,
as I can be a guide to them.

Offering of the gifts

Sung response

Invitation to the table:

This is not my table,
this is not the church's table,
this is the Lord's table –
and everyone is welcome:

those who get up every morning
to try to follow Jesus,
as well as those who fall asleep
remembering how they didn't;

those who know
what this meal is all about,
as well as those who struggle
with the mystery;

those whose faith overflows
the edges of their hearts,
as well as those
who run on empty.

So come, neighbour and stranger,
come, brother and sister,
come, old and young.
Come!
For you are God's beloved,
and welcome to this feast.

Communion song

Great prayer of thanksgiving:

May the God of mountaintops be with you!
AND ALSO WITH YOU!

People of God, lift up your hearts to the One who calls to you.
WE OPEN OUR HEARTS TO THE ONE WHO INVITES US TO LISTEN.

Beloved of God, offer praise to the One who is with you in this moment.
OUR VOICES UNITE IN THANKING OUR GOD WHO LOVES US.

Awesome Creator,
overshadowing chaos, you spoke:
and mountains were topped with mist,
singing brooks meandered through fields.

Created in your image,
but tempted by sin and death
who came to us
masked as life and joy,
we had the audacity
to demand our way.

You did not turn your face away,
sending the prophets into all
those ordinary places where we lived
to call us back to you.
Though they spoke boldly of your hope,
we did not listen to a single word.

So you sent Jesus, your glory,
to become flesh and blood
so we might be reshaped
as your beloved children.

With those in every time and place,
with those gathered here at this moment,
we sing of our joy to you:

HOLY, HOLY, HOLY! GOD WHO LISTENS TO OUR CRIES.
ALL CREATION TREMBLES WITH HOPE AND JOY.
HOSANNA IN THE HIGHEST!

BLESSED IS THE ONE WHO COMES WITH WORDS OF LIFE.
HOSANNA IN THE HIGHEST!

Holy are you, Wonders of wonders,
and your Beloved reigns in peace.

He set aside his glory
to load us down with the riches
of your grace and peace.

He silenced our silly complaints,
so we might hang on to every
word of hope, of joy.

He went to the cross,
ripping the mask off death,
so we could see the face
of an empty threat.

As we celebrate your Chosen,
as we prepare to listen to him with our lives,
we speak of that mystery we call faith:

CHRIST DIED:
TO PULL ASIDE THE CURTAIN OF DEATH.

CHRIST ROSE:
TO REVEAL THE PROMISE OF NEW LIFE.

CHRIST WILL COME:
TO SHOW US THE FACE OF GOD.

As we gather around your table,
pour out the blessings of your Spirit,
transforming these simple gifts
into that grace which changes lives.

As we feed upon the Word which is broken for us,
strength us to go forth to speak boldly:
reading a story to a lonely child,
advocating for the voiceless,
telling your good news to those who wander in despair.

As your Cup of peace fills us,
inspire us to go out into the world,
learning that where we do justice for
the oppressed and rejected,
we find ourselves in your presence.
So then, when all time comes to an end
and we are gathered in your glory
with our sisters and brothers
around the feast of grace and peace,
we will sing your grace forever and ever,
God in Community, Holy and One.
Amen

Prayers of concern

Communion

Song

Sending:

From glory's mountaintops of wonder and delight,
where we long to stay, we will go:
TAKING GOD'S GRACE INTO
THE SHADOWS OF THE WORLD.

Walking the valleys of everyday life,
where noise overwhelms us, we will journey:
LISTENING TO THE VOICES OF ALL
WHO ARE GOD'S PRESENCE FOR US.

In the mist of misguided living, we will walk:
FOLLOWING THE ONE WHO COMES
TO LEAD US DOWN PATHS OF HUMILITY.
AMEN

Music

Wild Goose Publications is part of the Iona Community:

- An ecumenical movement of men and women from different walks of life and different traditions in the Christian church
- Committed to the gospel of Jesus Christ, and to following where that leads, even into the unknown
- Engaged together, and with people of goodwill across the world, in acting, reflecting and praying for justice, peace and the integrity of creation
- Convinced that the inclusive community we seek must be embodied in the community we practise

Together with our staff, we are responsible for:

- Our islands residential centres of Iona Abbey, the MacLeod Centre on Iona, and Camas Adventure Centre on the Ross of Mull

and in Glasgow:
- The administration of the Community
- Our work with young people
- Our publishing house, Wild Goose Publications
- Our association in the revitalising of worship with the Wild Goose Resource Group

The Iona Community was founded in Glasgow in 1938 by George MacLeod, minister, visionary and prophetic witness for peace, in the context of the poverty and despair of the Depression. Its original task of rebuilding the monastic ruins of Iona Abbey became a sign of hopeful rebuilding of community in Scotland and beyond. Today, we are about 250 Members, mostly in Britain, and 1500 Associate Members, with 1400 Friends worldwide. Together and apart, 'we follow the light we have, and pray for more light'.

For information on the Iona Community contact:
The Iona Community, Fourth Floor, Savoy House, 140 Sauchiehall Street,
Glasgow G2 3DH, UK. Phone: 0141 332 6343
e-mail: admin@iona.org.uk; web: www.iona.org.uk

For enquiries about visiting Iona, please contact:
Iona Abbey, Isle of Iona, Argyll PA76 6SN, UK. Phone: 01681 700404
e-mail: ionacomm@iona.org.uk

Wild Goose Publications, the publishing house of the Iona Community established in the Celtic Christian tradition of Saint Columba, produces books, e-books, CDs and digital downloads on:

- holistic spirituality
- social justice
- political and peace issues
- healing
- innovative approaches to worship
- song in worship, including the work of the Wild Goose Resource Group
- material for meditation and reflection

For more information:

Wild Goose Publications
The Iona Community
21 Carlton Court, Glasgow, G5 9JP, UK

Tel. +44 (0)141 429 7281
e-mail: admin@ionabooks.com

or visit our website at
www.ionabooks.com
for details of all our products and online sales